PRAISE FOR *WE CANNOT BE SILENT*

"Albert Mohler is one of our nation's most brilliant and courageous Evangelical Christian thinkers. In *We Cannot Be Silent*, he explains to Bible-believing Christians of all traditions why it is our duty to speak out in defense of biblical and natural-law principles of sexual morality and marriage. To bear witness to Christ and the gospel in contemporary culture is to make oneself a 'sign of contradiction' to those powerful forces who equate 'progress' and 'social justice' with sexual license and what Pope Francis calls 'gender ideology.' And that is what we, as Christians, must do—no matter the cost to ourselves. With the future of the family—and, indeed, the very dignity of the human person—at stake, silence is not an option."

—Robert P. George, McCormick Professor of
Jurisprudence, Princeton University

"Dr. Albert Mohler reminds us that current debates over LGBQT issues are part of a broader sexual revolution that challenges biblical morality in fundamental ways. It is simply not possible to simultaneously remain silent and remain faithful to the Lord Jesus."

—D. A. Carson, research professor of New
Testament, Trinity Evangelical Divinity School;
president of The Gospel Coalition

"In this post-modern world, Dr. Albert Mohler is among the most articulate and fearless defenders of biblical truth. In *We Cannot Be Silent* he describes for us the rapidly shifting moral landscape and explains what it means for the church and the culture. And above all, he reminds us that our mission is to be faithful to uphold truth and share the gospel with a lost and dying world."

—Jim Daly, president of Focus on the Family

"The rare clarity and perception of Dr. Mohler is brilliantly on display in this book. The master craftsman in piecing together the puzzle parts of culture, politics, history, theology, and Scripture into a mosaic of truth and reality, he does it again! His coherent, convincing and compelling arguments on the dominant and overriding issue of sexual identity and behavior and the Christian response are essential wisdom for the believer to possess. Mohler thoroughly equips the reader to courageously face the fight against sin while compassionately wielding the gospel of grace."

—Dr. John MacArthur, pastor of Grace Community
Church and president of the Master's College and
Seminary

"'On Jordan's Stormy Banks I Stand' was a favorite hymn in the church of my youth. But it's hard to see the banks, much less continue to stand there, when you are in the midst of the storm. This book analyzes the sexual revolution that is radically changing our culture, not excluding large sectors of the Christian church. But Albert Mohler gives us more than a weather report here. He proposes a renewed theology of the body inherent in the biblical doctrine of the Incarnation as the basis for a countercultural ethic. Every pastor and every parent should read this book."

—Timothy George, founding dean of Beeson Divinity School of Samford University and a member of the editorial boards of *First Things, Books and Culture,* and *Christianity Today*

"Albert Mohler is one of the preeminent Christian intellectuals of the century. While many stammer with confusion in the wake of the cultural revolutions of our time, Dr. Mohler stands and speaks. In this book, he applies keen cultural analysis and ancient biblical wisdom to vexing questions of marriage and sexuality. This book will equip Christ's church to speak with moral clarity and to stand with gospel conviction."

—Russell Moore, president of the Ethics and Religious Liberty Commission, Southern Baptist Convention

"Few men in a generation can rise to the moment in the midst of a plurality of crises in the culture. Albert Mohler is one of these men. *We Cannot Be Silent* is a compelling call to each Christ-follower and church to not retreat, but to stand boldly and unashamedly upon God's Truth, but always with love and compassion. When you read this book, you will see the unique brilliance of a scholar and the vibrant fire of a man who is gripped by God himself. Read it and share it with the world."

—Dr. Ronnie Floyd, president of the Southern Baptist Convention and senior pastor of Cross Church

"This is one of the most useful books I've read in a long time. . . . The changes we've seen are more sudden and even more sweeping in their implications than we supposed. Yet these changes have roots stretching back for decades and more. . . . Student, freshman, campus worker, youth group leader, pastor, professor—read this book and study it with others."

—Mark Dever, pastor of Capitol Hill Baptist Church, Washington, DC, and president of 9Marks

"As a modern-day cultural apologist for the Christian faith, Albert Mohler is without peer. *We Cannot Be Silent* not only establishes biblical rectitude on the tough subjects that he addresses but also prepares the church to address these issues with the compassion and love of Christ. Mohler knows both intellectually and existentially the cost borne in suffering, and he prepares the reader for that inevitability as well. This book will bless and fortify your life and the life of your church."

—Paige Patterson, president of Southwestern Baptist
Theological Seminary, Fort Worth, Texas

"In this sobering yet gripping volume, Albert Mohler tells the cautionary tale of the same-sex and transgender revolutions that have transformed sexual morality and redefined marriage in the Western world faster than anyone could have imagined. Engaging in his vintage masterful cultural analysis, Mohler explores the future implications of this massive moral shift for church and society. Yet this book does more than merely provide information; it is a call to action, urging Christians to bear bold witness to the truth embedded uniquely in God's design for man and woman according to his Word."

—Andreas J. Köstenberger, coauthor (with Margaret
Köstenberger) of the *God's Design for Man and
Woman,* Biblical Foundations and BibleMesh
curriculum

"Dr. Mohler is known and appreciated for his Christ-centered insights on the intersection of Christianity and culture. Of particular value in this accessible work are his reflections on how heterosexual compromises in church and public policy led to acceptance of homosexual marriage, which in turn now threatens our religious liberty. His short answers to thirty hard questions in the last chapter will stimulate good discussion."

—Robert A. J. Gagnon, Ph.D., associate professor of
New Testament, Pittsburgh Theological Seminary
and author of *The Bible and Homosexual Practice* and
coauthor of *Homosexuality and the Bible: Two Views*

WE CANNOT BE SILENT

WE CANNOT BE SILENT

Speaking truth to a culture redefining sex, marriage, & the very meaning of right & wrong

R. Albert Mohler, Jr.

NELSON
BOOKS

An Imprint of Thomas Nelson

Published in Nashville, Tennessee, by Nelson Books, an imprint of Thomas Nelson. Nelson Books and Thomas Nelson are registered trademarks of HarperCollins Christian Publishing, Inc.

Published in association with the literary agency of Wolgemuth & Associates, Inc.

Thomas Nelson titles may be purchased in bulk for educational, business, fund-raising, or sales promotional use. For information, please e-mail SpecialMarkets@ThomasNelson.com.

Unless otherwise noted, Scripture quotations are taken from THE ENGLISH STANDARD VERSION. © 2001 by Crossway Bibles, a division of Good News Publishers.

Scripture quotations marked NASB are taken from the New American Standard Bible®. Copyright © 1960, 1962, 1963, 1968, 1971, 1972, 1973, 1975, 1977, 1995 by The Lockman Foundation. Used by permission. (www.Lockman.org)

Scripture quotations marked KJV are taken from the King James Version. Public domain.

Library of Congress Cataloging-in-Publication Data

Mohler, R. Albert, Jr., 1959-
  We cannot be silent: speaking truth to a culture redefining sex, marriage, and the very meaning of right and wrong / R. Albert Mohler, Jr.
    pages cm
  Includes bibliographical references and index.
  ISBN 978-0-7180-3248-7
  1. Marriage—Religious aspects—Christianity. 2. Sex—Religious aspects—Christianity. 3. Christianity and culture. I. Title.
  BT706.M64 2016
  261.8'35—dc23
                                    2015011732

Printed in the United States of America

15 16 17 18 19 RRD 6 5 4

Dedicated to the memory of my grandparents,
Montesco Jasper and Carrie English Johnson,
Russell Lester and Dorothy May Mohler,
who so loved me, and without whom I would not know who I am.

Only take care, and keep your soul diligently, lest you
forget the things that your eyes have seen, and lest they
depart from your heart all the days of your life. Make them
known to your children and your children's children.

—Deuteronomy 4:9 ESV

CONTENTS

PREFACE

One of my most vivid memories of childhood is standing with my grandfather, looking out on the landscape after a hurricane had passed through our town. Growing up in Florida, I knew to respect the great storms, but I was not prepared to see how much the landscape had been changed. I can remember thinking that I had underestimated the storm—a mistake I was determined not to make again.

Something similar is happening to many Christians in America today. We look out on the horizon around us and realize that our culture has been radically changed. In this case, the storm is a vast moral revolution, and that revolution is not even close to its conclusion. In fact, there will likely be no conclusion to this moral revolution within our lifetimes, or the lifetimes of our children and grandchildren.

We are now witnesses to a revolution that is sweeping away a sexual morality and a definition of marriage that has existed for thousands of years. This is the morality and understanding of marriage that has been central to societies shaped by biblical witness and the influence of both Judaism and Christianity. It is also important to note that throughout human history—in virtually all civilizations—marriage has been understood as the union of a man and a woman. That has changed.

This book is about this moral revolution, how it happened and what it means for us, for our churches, and for our children. It is important to trace the revolution and understand that the most heated controversies of our day did not emerge from a vacuum onto the daily headlines. Every revolution has a story, and the story of this revolution is one that we can now trace. To put the truth plainly, this revolution did not start with same-sex marriage, and it will not end there.

The revolution that is centered on transforming sexual morality and redefining marriage has succeeded faster than its most eager advocates had even imagined, as they themselves now admit. But this revolution could not have achieved such a velocity if the ground had not been cleared by developments that came long before same-sex marriage. We will look at what came before same-sex marriage, and we will look into the future to what may come after.

Every Christian church—and every Christian—will face huge decisions in the wake of this moral storm. When marriage is redefined, an entire universe of laws, customs, rules, and expectations changes as well. Words such as *husband* and *wife, mother* and *father,* at one time the common vocabulary of every society, are now battlegrounds of moral conflict. Just consider how children's picture books will have to change in the wake of this revolution. As those who demand this revolution make clear, there will be no model of a normative family structure left in its wake.

But this revolution has also reached into our churches. Some are arguing that Christians need to revise our sexual morality and the definition of marriage to avoid costly and controversial confrontations with the culture at large. Are they right?

In chapter 1 we trace the revolution and its vast impact. Like a hurricane on a radar screen, this massive moral shift can be seen in its development and its storm track. We cannot tell this story without looking at how secularized our society has become. It turns out that the secularizing of the culture is central to the moral shift.

In chapter 2 we look at the arrival of birth control and divorce, and at the fact that few Christians seemed to understand at the time that these developments were setting the stage for a total redefinition of marriage and the family. You can't have a sexual revolution without easy contraception and so-called "no fault" divorce. By the early 1970s, both were largely in place. Christians seemed to take little notice of either.

In chapter 3 the development of the homosexual movement is put within the context of that moral revolution. Those advocating for the normalization of same-sex relationships and behaviors built upon the momentum of the sexual revolution, and they did so with spectacular success.

Chapter 4 is a close look at same-sex marriage itself. How is it possible that marriage could be redefined to include a man married to another man or a woman married to another woman? We know that a majority of Americans now affirm what just a decade ago a vast majority rejected—the legalization of same-sex marriage. What does this mean? What *will* it mean?

Chapter 5 considers the transgender revolution. In the long run, the redefinition of sex and gender will have even more far-reaching consequences than the redefinition of marriage. Are there any limits to where the transgender revolution will lead? None are yet in sight.

Chapter 6 looks squarely at the end of marriage. What will marriage mean when virtually anyone has a "right" to marry? What *can* it mean? Some voices on both sides of the same-sex marriage controversy agree that, whatever else may happen, marriage will never be the same. Indeed, marriage as a privileged and respected institution—even as an expectation of normal adulthood—is disappearing before our eyes.

Chapter 7 asks a straightforward question: What does the Bible really say about sex? For biblical Christians, this is the most important question of all. We will look at the Bible's understanding of sex, gender, marriage, and morality. The Bible will establish the framework for our consideration of marriage, identity, and sexuality. As we will see, the Bible presents a clear understanding of sex, gender, and marriage as among God's greatest gifts to humanity—to be honored as he intended.

Chapter 8 looks at the very real and urgent challenges to religious liberty we now confront. These challenges jump right onto the headlines virtually every week, and the list of issues headed for courts and legislatures is long and getting longer. Will Christian colleges and universities be coerced into violating Christian conviction? Will individual Christians be denied their religious liberties? What will same-sex marriage mean for your church and its freedom?

Chapter 9 steps back to look at the sexual revolution—right down to the arrival of same-sex marriage—in light of the gospel of Jesus Christ. For Christians, the gospel is our constant frame of reference. In that light, the moral confusion of our day represents a real opportunity for courageous Christian witness. If we have confidence in the gospel, we will have confidence in the compassion of truth.

Chapter 10 is a consideration of pressing questions. Should a Christian attend a same-sex wedding? Is sexual orientation a choice? How do we balance truth and compassion? Would you allow your child to play at a home with two moms or two dads? Why do none of the ancient Christian creeds define marriage? Should government legislate morality? These are just a few of the questions now pressing upon us. How should we answer?

And finally, the book concludes with a "Word to the Reader" written in response to the Supreme Court's decision on gay marriage.

I remember standing with my grandfather and looking at a large boat lying on its side, far from the lake. I didn't have to ask how it got there. The hurricane explained everything.

We cannot understand our times without looking honestly at the moral hurricane sweeping across our culture, leaving very little untouched, if not radically changed, in its wake. But understanding is just a start. When it comes to marriage and morality, Christians cannot be silent—not because we are morally superior, but because we know that God has a better plan for humanity than we would ever devise for ourselves.

Beyond that, we cannot be silent because we know that Jesus Christ is Lord and that he came to save us from our sins. We cannot rightly tell people about the gospel of Jesus Christ if we do not speak rightly about sin and its consequences.

As I have said, I stood there with my grandfather, determined never to underestimate a hurricane again. We dare not underestimate the scale, scope, and significance of this moral revolution. Even more urgently, we cannot underestimate the gospel of Jesus Christ. This book is written in the hope that the church will be found faithful, even in the midst of the storm.

1

IN THE WAKE OF A REVOLUTION

The prophetic writer Flannery O'Connor rightly warned us years ago that we must "push as hard as the age that pushes against you."[1] This book is an attempt to do just that.

We are living in the midst of a revolution. The Christian church in the West now faces a set of challenges that exceeds anything it has experienced in the past. The revolution that has transformed most of Western Europe and much of North America is a revolution more subtle and more dangerous than revolutions faced in previous generations. This is a revolution of ideas—one that is transforming the entire moral structure of meaning and life that human beings have recognized for millennia.

This new revolution presents a particular challenge to Christianity, for a commitment to the authority of Scripture and to revealed truths runs into direct conflict with the central thrust of this revolution. Christians are not facing an isolated set of issues that cause us to be merely perplexed and, at times, at odds with the larger culture. We are instead facing a redefinition of marriage and transformation of the family. We are facing a complete transformation of the way human beings relate to one another in the most intimate contexts of life. We are facing nothing less than a comprehensive redefinition of life, love, liberty, and the very meaning of right and wrong.

This massive revolution is taking place across the entire cultural landscape, affecting virtually every dimension of life and demanding total acceptance of its claims and affirmation of its aims. Christians who are committed to faithfulness to the Bible as the Word of God and to the gospel as the only message of salvation must face this unavoidable challenge.

A Comprehensive Revolution

British theologian Theo Hobson has argued that the scale and scope of this challenge are unprecedented. According to critics of Hobson's argument, the challenge of the sexual revolution and the normalization of homosexuality is nothing new or unusual. Churches have always shown the ability to plod their way through hard moral issues before, and so they will again with homosexuality. Hobson himself confessed that he would have agreed with this line of reasoning at one point, but not anymore. For Hobson, the issue of homosexuality presents the church with a challenge it has never faced before.[2]

Why is this such a challenge to Christianity? Hobson has suggested that the first factor is the either-or quality of the new morality. There is no middle ground in the church's engagement with homosexuality. Either churches will affirm the legitimacy of same-sex relationships and behaviors or they will not.

Hobson's second factor is the new morality's rapid rate of success. The normalization of homosexuality—something regarded as "unspeakably immoral" for centuries—has happened at breakneck speed. It has happened so fast that homosexuality is now considered as a legitimate lifestyle, and one that deserves legal protection. Moreover, as Hobson argued, the speed of the new morality's success "has basically ousted traditionalist sexual morality from the moral high ground."[3]

In other words, the sexual revolution has actually turned the tables on Christianity. The Christian church has long been understood by the culture at large to be the guardian of what is right and righteous. But now the situation is fundamentally reversed. The culture generally identifies Christians as on the *wrong* side of morality. Those who hold to biblical teachings concerning human sexuality are now deposed from the position of high moral ground. This change is not simply "the waning of the taboo." As Hobson explained:

> The case for homosexual equality takes the form of a moral crusade. Those who want to uphold the old attitude are not just dated moralists (as is the case with those who want to uphold the old attitude to premarital sex or illegitimacy). They are accused of moral deficiency. The old taboo surrounding this practice does not disappear but "bounces back" at those who seek to uphold it. Such a sharp turn-around is, I think, without parallel in moral history.[4]

The moral revolution is now so complete that those who will not join it are understood to be deficient, intolerant, and harmful to society. What was previously understood to be immoral is now celebrated as a moral good. The church's historic teaching on homosexuality—shared by the vast majority of the culture until very recently—is now seen as a relic of the past and a repressive force that must be eradicated.

This explains why the challenge of the moral revolution poses such a threat to the whole of Christianity and to its position in modern societies. And yet even as we understand this revolution to be a new thing, its roots are not recent. As a matter of fact, the church has seen the sexual revolution taking place turn by turn for virtually all of the last century. What now becomes clear is that most Christians vastly underestimated the challenge the sexual revolution represents.

The Source of the Sexual Revolution: The Secularization of the Western Worldview

The background to this revolution is a great intellectual shift that occurred in concert with the secularization of Western societies. The modern age has brought many cultural benefits, but it has also brought a radical change in the way citizens of today's societies think, feel, relate, and make moral judgments. The Enlightenment's elevation of reason at the expense of revelation was followed by a radical anti-supernaturalism. From looking at Europe, it is clear that the modern age has alienated an entire civilization from its Christian roots, along with Christian moral and intellectual commitments. Scandinavian nations, for example, now register almost imperceptible levels of Christian belief. Increasingly, the same is true of both the Netherlands and Great Britain. Sociologists now speak openly of the death of Christian Britain—and the evidence of Christian decline is abundant throughout most of Europe. That same Christian decline has now come to America.

In 1983, Carl F. H. Henry described the future possibilities for Western societies:

> If modern culture is to escape the oblivion that has engulfed the earlier civilizations of man, the recovery of the will of the self-revealed God in the realm of justice and law is crucially imperative. Return to pagan misconceptions of divinized rulers, or a divinized cosmos, or to quasi-Christian conceptions of natural law or natural justice, will bring inevitable disillusionment. Not all pleas for transcendent authority truly serve God or man. By aggrandizing law and human rights and welfare to their sovereignty all manner of earthly leaders eagerly preempt the role of the divine and obscure the living God of scriptural revelation. The alternatives are clear: either we return to the God of the Bible or we perish in the pit of lawlessness.[5]

Regrettably, Henry's warning has gone unheeded and the path of American culture has become more and more secularized. *Secular* refers to the absence of any binding divine authority or belief. *Secularization* is a sociological process whereby societies become less theistic as they become more modern. As societies move into conditions of deeper and more progressive modernity, they move away from a binding force of religious belief, and theistic belief in particular.

Canadian philosopher Charles Taylor has compellingly portrayed the story of Western society's transition into secularism. In his book *A Secular Age*, Taylor described the pre-modern age as a time when it *was impossible not to believe*. In other words, belief in God had no intellectual alternatives in the West. There was no alternative set of explanations for the world and its operations, or for moral order. All that changed with the arrival of modernity. In the modern age, a secular alternative to Christian theism emerged and it became *possible not to believe*. But during this time theism was still intellectually and culturally viable. But, as Taylor noted, those days are behind us. In our own postmodern age it is now considered *impossible to believe*.

Significantly, Taylor pinpoints this unbelief as a lack of cognitive commitment to a self-existent, self-revealing God. Secularization is not about rejecting all religion. In fact, even hyper-secularized Americans often consider themselves to be religious or spiritual. Secularization, according to Taylor, is about the rejection of a belief in a *personal* God, one who holds and exerts authority.[6]

The implications of this worldview shift are massive. For example, in light of these current intellectual conditions, sociologist Mary Eberstadt has noted that "it is surely the case in large stretches of the advanced West today, many sophisticated people do not believe that the churches have any authority *whatsoever* to dictate constraints on individual freedom."[7]

This may be true, but the church cannot abdicate its responsibility for Christian truth-telling in a postmodern age. The secular conditions make it more challenging and difficult, even seemingly impossible at times. Our culture is growing more and more resistant to a God—any god—who would speak to us with words such as "Thou shalt" and "Thou shalt not." The fact that Christians enter every conversation as believers in the Lord Jesus Christ who are bound by biblical revelation means that society will label us as the intellectual outlaws—breaking the rules of engagement by appealing to a personal Creator and divine authority.

Yet explicit Christian truth-telling is the church's reason for being. As Peter wrote, "But you are a chosen race, a royal priesthood, a holy nation, a people for his own possession, that you may proclaim the excellencies of him who called you out of darkness into his marvelous light" (1 Peter 2:9). The God of the Bible has sent his church into the world to tell the truth about himself—about his laws and commands, about his grace and love, and most important, about the gospel of Jesus Christ.

The American Sex Revolution

Today we are witnessing nothing less than a total revolution in sexual morality. And a moral revolution is dramatically more important than mere moral shift. Moral shifts happen all around us and can regularly result in positive cultural transitions. For example, as someone who grew up in the 1960s, I can remember positive, comedic depictions of drunken behavior on television. But Otis the benevolent drunk on *The Andy Griffith Show* would be impossible to present in the mainstream media today. This is due to the important shift in moral judgment concerning alcohol and drunk driving. A successful anti–drunk driving campaign has turned what was thought in the 1950s to be a minor indiscretion to what is now understood, quite properly, to be a major crime. The eventual heightened criminalization and moral sanction against drunk driving was the result of a society coming face-to-face with horrible damages caused by drunk driving.

This kind of moral change happens on any number of issues, but in a way that can be absorbed within the general moral trajectory of a culture. In other words, *moral change* generally takes a rather long period of time, and in a way that is consistent with a culture's moral commitments.

A *moral revolution* represents the exact opposite of that pattern. What we are now experiencing is not the logical outworking of the West's Christian-influenced teachings on human sexuality, but the repudiation of them. This is a fundamentally different type of moral change and represents a challenge that is leaving many Christians confused and befuddled, some angry and anxious, and others asking hard questions about how the church should respond in such a time of crisis.

All this has to be put into the larger context of changes that have transformed the way most people in Western societies *think*. The moral revolution is part of a seismic shift in Western culture that has occurred during the last two centuries. In that span of time vast social changes have transformed the way people in advanced industrialized economies live, relate to one another, and engage the larger world. If that sounds like an overstatement, just consider the fact that at the beginning of the twentieth century most Americans lived in a rural context as part of an extended family and with a range of geographic mobility that was generally confined to a very small area. The idea that human beings would be flung coast to coast in an advanced economy and that work would be transformed from the tilling of the soil to what is now described as "knowledge work" is something that would have been inconceivable. These cultural transformations have uniquely impacted the family, which has been stripped of many of its defenses and separated from the larger context of kinship and the extended family.

An article in *Bloomberg Businessweek* about changing patterns in the American diet also demonstrates how moral revolutions can take place so quickly. As the authors explained, "cultural shifts don't happen overnight. They build slowly—a sip of coconut water here, a quinoa purchase there, and suddenly the American diet looks drastically different than it did 10 years ago."[8] Indeed, most of us can recognize this just by looking at our own dinner tables.

But now imagine that same process expanded into the realm of morality and the major issues of life. In truth, the same kind of process has taken place. Just as changes in the diet take place without often being perceived, the same is true of the vast shift in morality that is taking place all around us—and we cannot say we were not warned.

Writing back in 1956, Pitirim Sorokin sounded an alarm about what he called "the American Sex Revolution." Sorokin, the first professor of sociology and later head of that department at Harvard University, was a moral prophet. As a member of the intellectual elite at Harvard, Sorokin represented the mainstream moral understanding of America at the time, and he was profoundly alarmed at the sexual revolution he saw taking place all around him.

> Among the many changes of the last few decades a peculiar revolution has been taking place in the lives of millions of American men and women. Quite different from the better-known political and economic revolutions, it goes almost unnoticed. Devoid of noisy public explosions, its stormy scenes are confined to the privacy of the bedroom and involve only individuals. Unmarked by dramatic events on a large scale, it is free from civil war, class struggle, and bloodshed. It has no revolutionary army to fight its enemies. It does not try to overthrow governments. It has no great leader; no hero plans it and no polit bureau directs it. Without plan or organization, it is carried on by millions of individuals, each acting on his own. *As a revolution*, it has not been featured on the front pages of our press, or on radio or television. Its name is the sex revolution.[9]

There is a particular power to Sorokin's use of the word *revolution*. In a way most of us cannot even conceive, Sorokin knew how revolutions happened and the carnage they often left in their wake. Born in Russia, Sorokin was condemned to death by the last emperor, Czar Nicholas II. Escaping that death sentence, he later served as private secretary to the interim government that was in place after the death of the czar. Sentenced to death once again, he was eventually exiled by Vladimir Lenin—an event that prompted his move to the United States and eventually to Harvard University. In other words, Sorokin used the word *revolution* to make a point that no other word would convey. Even in 1956, he saw the world being turned upside down; he saw the sexual revolution coming in full force.[10]

The idea of a sexual revolution can be traced back to the nineteenth century when intellectuals in Europe began to push back against the inherited sexual morality that had come into Western civilization through the Christian tradition. Fueled with a desire to redefine love and sex for a new age, these intellectuals argued that Christian sexual morality was inherently repressive and that true liberty could only come to human beings if the sexual morality derived from the Bible was overthrown and subverted.

For the most part, calls for a sexual revolution in the nineteenth century were primarily confined to a class of self-consciously liberal intellectuals who lived mostly on the fringes of the establishment cultures in Europe and the United States. All that began to shift in the twentieth century as vast changes in Western societies occurred with the cataclysms of two world wars, the new industrial age, and the rise of a general spirit of revolution. In a fairly short span of time, many of the ideas that had been limited to an intellectual fringe were discussed in more mainstream sectors of society. The academic world also began to pay serious attention to these transformations, driven by a significant turn toward individual autonomy and the idea that many of the problems faced by modern human beings were actually caused by the repressive presence of the Christian moral tradition.

In the United States, the twentieth century began with laws in place in virtually every community that criminalized forms of sexual behavior considered aberrant. These communities also recognized marriage between a man and a woman as the only proper context for sexual behavior, procreation, and the raising of children. Fast-forward to the end of the twentieth century, and pornography is so pervasive that it is just a click away from the nearest computer screen. The legal definition of obscenity is now almost impossible to violate, and the local newsstand offers sexually explicit material in the form of mainstream entertainment. Legal codes have been redefined so that the only operational issue in the criminalization of sexual behavior is the element of consent. In the main, the decriminalization of what had been considered aberrant sexual behaviors was virtually complete by the first years of the twenty-first century.

Another interesting development in all this is that the sexual revolution was so utterly successful that most Americans living today do not even recognize that it happened. Yet a comparison of American culture in 1950 with today reveals that the sexual revolution has reached almost every corner of the culture and every dimension of life. As Lillian B. Rubin observed in her book *Erotic Wars: What Happened to the Sexual Revolution?*:

> In the public arena, sex screams at us from every turn—from our television and movie screens, from the billboards on our roadways, from the pages of our magazines, from the advertisements for goods, whether they seek to sell automobiles, soap or undergarments. Bookstore shelves bulge with volumes about sex, all of them dedicated to telling us what to do and how to do it. TV talk shows feature solemn discussions of pornography, impotence, premarital sex, marital

sex, extramarital sex, group sex, swinging, sadomasochism, and as many of the other variations of sexual behavior their producers can think of, whether the ordinary or bizarre. Even the comic strips offer graphic presentations of every aspect of adult sexuality.[11]

What Drives the Sexual Revolution?

The twentieth century will be recognized as the century of the greatest change in sexual morality in the history of Western civilization. But, even as our own century is plowing new ground of moral revolution, the fact remains that the seeds were planted in the twentieth century. The question remains, how did all this happen?

We have already seen that the sexual revolution did not emerge in a vacuum. Modern societies created a context for moral revolution that had never been available before. Certain cultural conditions had to prevail in order for the revolution to get the traction it needed to succeed.

One of these factors was the rise of urbanization. As odd as it may seem, even as the city is a concentration of human beings, it actually offers an unprecedented opportunity for anonymity. Many observers of the sexual revolution point to the fact that, from the very beginning, the sexual revolution was a *cosmopolitan* revolution—emerging first in cities and then spreading out to the rest of the culture.

Similarly, technological advances fueled the sexual revolution. Contraceptive technology, in particular, has spurred the velocity of the sexual revolution. Put bluntly, so long as sex between a man and a woman implied the possibility of pregnancy, there was a biological check on extramarital sexual activity. Once the Pill arrived, with all its promises of reproductive control, the biological check on sexual immorality that had shaped human existence from Adam and Eve forward was removed almost instantaneously.

Closely related to these advances in contraceptive technology was the arrival of "sex experts." The so-called research of Alfred Kinsey or the Masters and Johnson team gave the sexual revolution the air of scientific authority.[12] Kinsey's research, for example, was touted by the intellectual elites in America as proof that Americans were actually living by a moral code that was already diametrically opposed to what Christianity taught. But Kinsey's research was fraudulent from the start—"an outright deception," according to author Sue Browder. Nevertheless, as Browder noted, in the last fifty years, "Kinseyism" has been used "to sway court decisions, pass legislation, introduce sex education into our schools, and even push for a redefinition of marriage."[13]

The revolution also required massive alterations in the law. A legal revolution was needed to revise laws that restricted sexual behavior and criminalized certain conduct. The same revolution in the law would eventually redefine marriage itself in order to remove it as the central expectation and boundary for all legitimate sexual relationships.

By the middle of the 1970s, most of the legal groundwork for the sexual revolution had been accomplished in the United States. Virtually all that remained was the normalization of homosexuality. The Supreme Court struck down all criminal laws prohibiting consensual same-sex behavior in the 2003 case *Lawrence v. Texas*. Then, in 2013, it struck down the federal government's definition of marriage as exclusively the union of a man and a woman in *United States v. Windsor*. Thus, by the year 2013, very little remained of the correspondence between American law and the moral convictions that had shaped the society just a century before.

This revolution in the law was preceded by a revolution in American academic thought that fueled the future decisions handed down by the courts. During the 1930s and '40s, even before the advent of the Kinsey reports, professors and leading intellectuals in America began to speak of the inherited sexual morality as repressive, echoing fringe voices recognized as dangerously radical just a half century before. Oddly enough, even as the United States entered a period of tremendous family stability in the aftermath of the Second World War, the intellectual foundations were so shaken that, by the end of the 1950s, leading academics were speaking of the natural family and living in the suburbs as the example of what Americans should recognize as an artificial existence, shaped by a repressive sexual morality and false cultural expectations.

By the 1990s, the most respected mainstream academic institutions in America featured academic departments that were devoted entirely to the study and promotion of the strangest and most exotic theories of human sexuality—and often their practice as well. Many of these academics and intellectuals argued that all morality was merely socially constructed and was generally put in place by repressive authorities in order to preserve their power. Thus, the impulse toward liberation that was recognized as driving the dynamic toward democracy in much of the world was extended to morality with the explicit argument that those who were identified as "sexual minorities" must be liberated as part of the project of democracy and liberty.

And of course, these new ideologies ultimately trickled down into high schools and even into grade schools. By the time the average American child graduates from a public school in the United States, he has been bombarded with the propaganda of the moral revolutionaries. In many school systems and districts, parents do not even have an "opt out" provision to remove their children from these sex education programs.

Of course, none of this would have been possible if Christianity had maintained a vital voice and the ability to speak prophetically to the larger culture concerning matters of marriage, sex, and morality. Nevertheless, the process of secularization had so shaped Western societies by the end of the twentieth century, and the United States in particular, that the moral authority of the Christian church was largely neutralized, certainly among the cultural and intellectual elites. Even as the vast majority of Americans would continue to identify as Christians in some way, it was clear that the restraining power of biblical morality no longer had the respect of the larger society and of those who had the greatest influence in the elite sectors of the nation. By the second decade of the twenty-first century, the Pew Research Center would report that fully 20 percent of Americans list "none" as their religious identification, and this increased to 30 percent among younger Americans.[14] Furthermore, younger Americans, those most intensely shaped by the moral revolution, would indicate a growing distancing from Christianity and its morality and a greater acceptance of the norms of the sexual revolution.

The Sexual Revolution and the Death of Morality

The postmodern quest for sexual emancipation cannot be neutral when it comes to the teachings of the Bible and the moral witness of historic Christianity. The inevitable collision between the two becomes very clear when we listen to the sexual revolutionaries. For example, John Heidenry, who traces what he calls "the rise and fall of the sexual revolution," looks to the future and argues:

> The road to sexual emancipation, though long and difficult, is not endless. Someday we will find the courage to declare that freedom of sexual expression does not mean merely a license to cast off sexual inhibitions. Rather it means the freedom to love another person on a consensual adult basis without fear of penalty or recrimination. Such freedom implies that sex is morally neutral—a position increasingly being adopted by enlightened elements within the Christian and Judaic traditions. . . . Finally, universal freedom of sexual expression means that no one sexual group has any claim to the moral high

ground, nor has it any basis regulating the consensual adult sexual behavior of any other group.[15]

The most important aspect of Heidenry's argument is the fact that he believes the sexual revolution cannot be complete until there is no "moral high ground" held by any form of sexual morality so long as adults are involved and they consent to the activity. In his view, any morality that goes beyond that is false and oppressive. Also note the fact that he points to what he identified as "enlightened elements within the Christian and Judaic traditions" as helping to fuel his revolution. Of course, those "enlightened elements" are the elements that are seeking to hollow out the central teachings and core of Christianity and Judaism, leaving nothing but the sexual revolution and moral relativism to remain.

And that takes us back to where we began—Theo Hobson's observation that the moral revolution we now face presents the Christian church with what he sees as a nearly insurmountable challenge because the current situation in the culture appears to call for the virtual abandonment of everything Christians have known from the Bible and everything the Christian church has taught for two thousand years. Understanding the challenge before us is a necessary first step, but the Christian church is called not only to understand the challenge but to respond to it in faithfulness. As Flannery O'Connor rightly warned, our responsibility is to "push as hard as the age that pushes against you." That's going to require a monumental act of faithfulness for the Christian church in this generation, but as we must clearly understand, anything less will mean the abandonment of Christianity.

2

IT DIDN'T START WITH SAME-SEX MARRIAGE

Opposition to the Christian understanding of sex and marriage did not begin with the arrival of same-sex marriage. Long before those in same-sex relationships had any realistic hope for the legal recognition of their unions, heterosexuals in the modern age seemed to be accomplishing the weakening and structural compromise of marriage all on their own. To understand this, we have to first take a look at some of the major intellectual and cultural shifts that led to the collapse of Christian morality among heterosexuals.

Any consideration of the eclipse of marriage in the last century must take into account four massive developments: birth control and contraception, divorce, advanced reproductive technologies, and cohabitation. All four of these together are required to facilitate the sexual revolution as we know it today. The redefinition of marriage could not have happened without these four developments

Birth Control and Contraception

The arrival of modern contraception changed human history, and the sexual revolution was fueled by the separation of sex from procreation. A number of evangelicals simply consider birth control and contraceptive technology to be features of the modern age that can be used without much moral or biblical reflection. This was not always the case. In fact, the use of birth control was condemned by every single Christian denomination at the beginning of the twentieth century. If that statement shocks you, just consider the scale of the moral revolution that is reflected in your surprise.

Historically, the Christian church condemned birth control because it has always sought to uphold the worth and dignity of children. Christians have consistently understood that children are, in every circumstance, a divine gift. This affirmation was so central to Christianity throughout the centuries that the issues of birth control, abortion, and infanticide were largely considered to be one and the same. The Christian church has always been concerned to promote the notion that children are to be welcomed and that any failure to welcome a child is itself an act of unfaithfulness.

The first church to break with the Christian tradition by affirming birth control and contraception was the Church of England. The 1930 Lambeth Conference, the periodic gathering of the bishops of the Church of England and the Anglican Communion, provided the context for the emergence of arguments for the acceptance of birth control. These arguments grew out of the church's desire to respond to the unique challenges posed by the modern age, the teeming population of British cities, and the demand of couples for increasing control over their reproductive destinies.

Concerns about overpopulation, largely driven by the theories of Thomas Malthus, led many to fear that the world would die of starvation due to increasing population. These fears that continue to be driven by a moral regime that is actively *antinatalist*—committed to lowering the birth rate. This flies in the face of the fact that the real demographic challenge of our times is an aging population with too *few* births rather than too many.

Early social observers also pointed to poverty in great cities such as London and suggested that birth control was necessary in order to limit the spread of social pathologies. In the United States, similar arguments were made by figures such as Margaret Sanger, who founded the organization eventually known as Planned Parenthood. But Sanger, along with so many of the other early activists for birth control, was driven by the theory of eugenics—an openly racist worldview and movement that operated by the motto "More from the fit, less from the unfit."[1] The inherent racism behind the population control movement—and abortion—is now a horrible embarrassment to the birth control movement. Nevertheless, it was one of the arguments that offered political momentum and assistance to the demand that birth control be normalized and legalized.

In the United States, most Protestant denominations resisted the temptation to endorse birth control and contraception, though several of the more liberal denominations had begun to accommodate the birth control mentality by the mid-twentieth century. Evangelicals, for the most part, simply ignored the issue. The energies of evangelical Christians had been devoted to so many other moral issues that birth control largely escaped focused attention. This set the stage for conservative Christians to be essentially co-opted by the contraceptive revolution when it took place, driven by the development and availability of "the Pill" in the early 1960s. It is shocking now to look back and see how little conversation took place among evangelicals at that time.

One major development in the Christian conversation took place when Pope Paul VI released his encyclical *Humanae Vitae* in 1968. The pope surprised and disappointed many Catholics who believed that the Catholic Church would answer the contraception question with at least a modified allowance of artificial birth control. Instead, the pope definitively closed the door on any artificial birth control, declaring that Catholic couples must be open to the gift of children in each and every occasion of sexual intercourse. The Catholic Church based its moral reasoning upon the classical Christian tradition and the Catholic appropriation of natural law. Evangelicals, forced at least in part by questions raised by the new definition of the Catholic position, seemed to be largely thankful that they had no pope to make such a declaration. Most evangelicals seemed to think that birth control was a Roman Catholic preoccupation and that evangelicals should not understand contraception to come with any urgent theological or moral questions. And yet it was evangelicals, not Roman Catholics, who were stepping outside of the Christian mainstream when it came to approving artificial birth control.[2]

Ultimately, the availability of birth control in a reliable form—particularly in the form of the Pill—unleashed the sexual revolution. So long as sex was predictably related to the potential of pregnancy, a huge biological check on sex outside of marriage functioned as a barrier to sexual immorality. Once that barrier was removed, sex and children became effectively separated and sex became redefined as an activity that did not have any necessary relation to the gift of children. It is impossible to exaggerate the importance of the separation of sex and babies from the moral equation.

Birth control also became the occasion for more radical changes that enabled and fueled the sexual revolution. When restrictions on access to birth control were challenged in the legal sphere, yet another avenue was opened to advance the sexual revolution. Most importantly, the U.S. Supreme Court's decision in *Griswold v. Connecticut* (1965) declared that *married* Americans had a right to access to birth control under the right to privacy, claimed to be assured by the Constitution. In his famous opinion, Justice William O. Douglas acknowledged that no such right was to be found in any explicit form within the text of the Constitution, but he claimed to have found the right to privacy, including the right to access to birth control, in what he defined as "penumbras" that were "formed by emanations from those guarantees that help give them life and substance."[3]

That strange legal language became the recipe that drove the sexual revolution forward at warp speed. Justice Douglas "found" a right to privacy in the sexual sphere that no previous generation believed was on the minds of the framers of the Constitution in any sense. He acknowledged, quite straightforwardly, that the right he had found within the Constitution was not found in its actual words. That is why he had to speak of "penumbras" and "emanations" coming from the Constitution.

To understand just how this fueled the sexual revolution, consider how that same kind of legal reasoning led to the court's "finding" of a woman's right to an abortion or of a same-sex couple's right to marry. This huge shift in American law had precursors to be sure, but we can look back to contraception as the key issue in the *Griswold* case in order to understand how the courts became the major engines of sexual revolution.

The moral revolution on the issue of contraception was fueled further just seven years later, when in 1972 the Supreme Court handed down the case of *Eisenstadt v. Baird*. This decision overturned a Massachusetts law that prohibited the prescription and distribution of birth control to *unmarried* couples. Clearly, the Supreme Court had now marginalized marriage, and the marital union was no longer the template for the moral context of legitimate sexual activity in the United States. So, add the development of birth control to the legal energies of the U.S. Supreme Court and the recipe for a moral revolution was nearly complete.

In more recent years, many evangelicals have begun to reconsider the morality of birth control and contraception and, on the positive side, have come to affirm the unconditional goodness of the gift of children. Even when evangelicals do not accept the Catholic admonition that each and every act of marital sex must be equally open to the gift of children, at the very least, evangelicals must affirm that every *marriage* must be open to the gift of children and that, should pregnancy occur, it is to be seen as an unconditional gift rather than as an imposition. However, the lack of serious evangelical engagement with the arrival of birth control set the stage for evangelical failure on an even larger level, and that failure is tied to the issue of divorce.

Divorce

Like birth control, divorce was inconceivable for most Christians throughout the history of the Christian church. Where it was legally available, it was under the most restrictive conditions in which some guilt (usually adultery) had to be assigned to one party or the other that would, on credible legal grounds, justify a divorce. Thus, without any apology, courts rooted in the Western tradition treated marriage with such respect that the dissolution of marriage required a legal process that was complicated and often excruciating. But these difficult legal processes were not without purpose. They were intended to make a point about the value of marriage and the disaster that every marital breakup represents. Indeed, as the writer Pat Conroy once stated, every divorce is "the death of a small civilization."[4] The Christian church, joined by the secular state, had for centuries affirmed the larger civilization's responsibility to protect every one of those smaller civilizations.

As the twentieth century dawned, however, theories of sexual liberation and developments in the law began to point toward a potential loosening of the restrictions on legal divorce. During the same period, many people, aided and abetted by the legal system, basically adopted a form of hypocrisy, admitting or imputing certain fault on legal grounds in order to obtain a divorce. At the same time, when the trauma of divorce produced a trial, it was, as the critics of existing divorce law often asserted, a truly grueling process filled with human misery.

During the 1960s, work to make divorce more readily available and to remove the stigma and the pain of the judicial process, led to the development of what became known as *no-fault* divorce. No-fault divorce was sold to the populace as a humanizing effort to allow marriages that were declared "irretrievably broken" to be terminated without the necessity of a court trial, painful testimony, and some finding of guilt. The first major no-fault divorce law was signed into effect by then governor Ronald Reagan in California in 1969. Reagan, who had been divorced, saw traditional divorce law as inhumane and thus saw no-fault divorce as a more humane means of dealing with marital strife.

Nevertheless, it soon became clear that the advent of no-fault divorce meant that the contraceptive revolution was followed by yet another revolutionary wave. The consequences for marriage were catastrophic. No-fault divorce, soon available in one form or another in virtually every state, became the norm in the United States by the end of the twentieth century. The divorce rate skyrocketed, leading to pathologies that the "humane" endorsers of no-fault divorce had either not foreseen or not adequately considered.

For example, the arrival of no-fault divorce, easily obtainable and in many cases uncontestable by a spouse, led not only to the breakup of families but also to a pandemic of abandoned children. The devastating effects on children—and on boys in particular—caused by absentee fathers is now well known and well documented. Furthermore, in almost every case, fathers generally found themselves in stronger economic positions five years after the divorce. In contrast, the wife and children left behind in the wake of no-fault divorce were most often left economically disadvantaged.

Ultimately, no-fault divorce became, whether acknowledged or not, a way of making every single marriage provisional. Marriage was thus shifted from being a covenant into being a mere contract and, as many of the proponents of easy divorce made clear, a contract "just like any other" that should be considered in force only insofar and for so long as both parties feel equally committed to the contract. But as an analysis of marriage throughout history makes clear, marriage has never worked solely as a contract. It only endures and serves its purposes within human society if it is understood as a covenant that requires the commitment not only of the man and the woman who enter it but of the entire civilization to respect and protect it from invasion, from subversion, and from being undermined by forces either from within or without.

Regrettably, if the society failed with the challenge of divorce, the Christian church failed even more inexcusably. The secular world may have looked at the Western legal tradition as something that could be amended or changed according to modern moral standards and popular demand, but Christians, supposedly bound to Scripture and the enduring truths of Christianity, should have understood that the divorce revolution flew directly in the face of clear biblical teachings. No-fault divorce is a rejection of the scriptural understanding of covenant that stands at the very heart of the Christian gospel. Nevertheless, Christian churches generally surrendered to the divorce rate revolution and abdicated their moral and biblical responsibility to uphold marriage in its covenantal essence.

Many factors were behind this failure. On the one hand, increasing numbers of Christian churches and denominations, surrendering to the larger ethic of personal autonomy, abdicated the responsibility of church discipline. In the same way that so many secular authorities had argued for no-fault divorce as a way of overcoming the hypocrisy of the older system of divorce law, many Christians began to advocate the abandonment of biblical church discipline because of the hypocrisy that sometimes corrupted that process. But destroying marriage is too high a price to pay for avoiding the risk of hypocrisy.

Another factor behind the evangelical surrender to the divorce culture was the close alignment of Christianity and cultural Christianity. From a theological perspective, the problem of cultural Christianity is that the culture always predominates over the Christianity. Divorce became a prime example of the fact that when the culture lost its mind on marriage, far too many churches decided to join the irrationality. Thus, evangelical churches began to treat divorce as a nonissue, even as the Bible includes the strongest statements imaginable about the permanence of marriage and the sinfulness of divorce. In fact, in one of the strongest statements found in Scripture, God declared that he "hates" divorce (Mal. 2:16 NASB).

God gave marriage to his human creatures as one of his greatest gifts, but he intended it as a covenant, not merely as a contract. The old language of *The Book of Common Prayer*, which continues to echo throughout wedding ceremonies to this day, includes the command "those whom God hath joined together let no man put asunder." Nevertheless, scores of pastors who repeated those words at the end of every wedding ceremony turned a blind eye when members of their own congregation violated that commitment by seeking and obtaining divorce.

To put the matter in the clearest possible terms, the evangelical abdication of responsibility for divorce set the stage for a loss of evangelical credibility to speak to the larger issue of sexuality and marriage. Quite pointedly, the church now has massive liabilities in terms of credibility when it seeks to speak about the "clear teachings of the Bible" on marriage.

Of course, failure in one area should not be followed by failure in another, but a sense of moral responsibility must weigh heavily upon the evangelical conscience. We must recognize that we, and many evangelicals before us, have sown the seeds for the very problems we now face. As the Scripture warns, those who sow the wind will reap the whirlwind (Hos. 8:7), and evangelicals of this generation are witnesses to the bitter taste of that word of judgment. In the end, we will almost surely have to concede that divorce will harm far more lives and cause far more direct damage than same-sex marriage. This is no argument for the legalization of same-sex marriage (which is an unmitigated disaster), but it is an acknowledgment that Christian failure on the issue of divorce helped open the door for the same-sex revolution.

Advanced Reproductive Technologies

Another major social shift with huge moral consequences was the development of advanced reproductive technologies. In one sense, this is the parallel development to the Pill and contraception. The arrival of modern contraceptives separated sex from babies, allowing couples to have sex, whether in marriage or not, without the "threat" of pregnancy. As we have seen, the moral implications of that new technology went far beyond the redefinition of the marital relationship. On the other side of the reproductive equation, the arrival of advanced reproductive technologies has allowed persons to have babies without having sex. So the Pill allowed sex without babies, and the modern reproductive technologies allow babies without sex. But this is not where the revolution ends, because in allowing babies without sex, the advanced reproductive technologies also allow persons who are biologically unable to have children to "have" children by some other means—and that goes far beyond heterosexual couples desiring children. It has enabled same-sex couples and single persons to "have" children, but not by moral means of procreation.

Once again, we need to understand that this revolution affected moral judgments and convictions far beyond those who were actually employing or considering the employment of these advanced reproductive technologies. The arrival of in vitro fertilization (IVF), preimplantation diagnostic tests, embryo sorting, surrogate motherhood, and other technologies redefined the very notion of what it meant to "have" a baby for all persons living in advanced nations.

The bottom line is this: Throughout all human history, until the most recent period, "having" a baby required a man and a woman in the act of sex. Babies were inseparable from the marital act and, as millennia of human experience demonstrated, having sex meant, quite regularly, having babies.

But the redefinition of all relationships was driven by the knowledge that sex between a man and a woman was now no longer necessary in order to produce a child. By the second decade of the twenty-first century, the combination of in vitro fertilization, donor insemination, a commercial gamete market for sperm and eggs, and pervasive availability of surrogate motherhood, allowed persons, single and coupled, heterosexual and homosexual, to "have" a child—and the larger public culture insists that all of this has come about with no great moral significance whatsoever.

Cohabitation: Sex Outside of Marriage

In previous centuries, nonmarital cohabitation between a man and a woman was not only frowned upon, it was sometimes even illegal. Furthermore, most societies found a way of turning lasting cohabitating unions into some form of marriage, whether the individuals wished to consider themselves married or not—thus the tradition in the United States and Great Britain of so-called common-law marriages. Additionally, sex outside of marriage, whether or not the couple lived together, was so morally sanctioned that the revelation of premarital or extramarital sex almost immediately led to grief, guilt, and the censure of society.

But just as society grew weary of sanctioning divorce and birth control, it also became lax in policing sex outside of marriage as well. Marriage itself became more and more marginalized to the moral equation of sex such that in vast sectors of our society today, the old references to "premarital sex" make no sense at all, since marriage is not even on the horizon.

That is a fundamentally new thing in terms of the way human beings have lived through millennia. As we shall see in later sections of this book, every single civilization has found its way to marriage, and usually quite quickly. Marriage has been established as the norm, the expectation, the mark of adulthood, and as the only socially sanctioned context for sexual intercourse and procreation. All that has changed in the last several decades, reversing millennia of moral conviction and social judgment.

Many Americans would consider the assumption that young people should save sex until marriage to be not only repressive but also downright irrational. The sex education regime, the moral revolutionaries, the advertising industry, and the entertainment industry have all conspired to suggest that marriage need not have anything at all to do with sex. All that remains is the morality of consent.

This abdication of marriage has turned America's college and university campuses into carnivals of a "hookup" culture. Furthermore, we are now faced by ample evidence that many American high schools are becoming similar contexts for this kind of rampant sexual behavior. Adding insult to injury, our government now insists upon the availability of birth control, including the "morning-after pill," to teenage girls, even without parental notification or permission. Incredibly, girls who could not obtain aspirin or penicillin without parental permission are now able, without parental notification, to obtain contraceptives.

Within the first decade of the twenty-first century, rates of extramarital sex and cohabitation had risen to levels experienced by no previous human society. Many Americans now live with marriage completely off their radar. In 2012, the *New York Times* reported that for women under age thirty, most births now occur outside of marriage.[5] The *Times* also reported, "Among mothers of all ages, a majority—59 percent in 2009—are married when they have children. But the surge of births outside marriage among younger women—nearly two-thirds of children in the United States are born to mothers under 30—is both a symbol of the transforming family and a hint of coming generational change."[6] This article also noted a clear and devastating correlation between out-of-wedlock births and pathologies of all kinds—ranging from children falling into poverty, failing to graduate from school, being arrested for crimes, or suffering from emotional and behavioral problems.[7]

Furthermore, in recent years, cohabitation before marriage has become not only expected but also a replacement for marriage itself. Karen Benjamin Guzzo of Bowling Green State University has observed that for millions of American young people, cohabitation is no longer a step toward getting married but rather a *replacement* for marriage as an ultimate expectation. In other words, fewer cohabitating couples are ever arriving at the altar.[8] Perhaps the most shocking aspect of Guzzo's research is her suggestion that cohabitation has not only replaced marriage but also replaced dating in the romantic lives of American young people. Relating to one another as a young man and a young woman without sexual activity is simply inconceivable to many young people, who consider the lack of openness to sex to be evidence of a lack of interest.

That development sweeps away not only thousands of years of moral knowledge but also an entire culture in which courtship was understood to be the proper means of arriving at marriage. Courtship involved not only the young man and the young woman, but also two families in a larger community, all of whom were expected to be a part of affirming the union and pledging to honor and support it. Cohabitation not only fails the test of endurance, but also requires none of the commitments that had made marriage such a stabilizing institution in society.

In a final observation about the lack of moral sanction against sex outside of marriage, we simply have to note the tremendous shift on the sinfulness of adultery that is taking place in America at large. Throughout the centuries, not only was adultery seen as sinful, it was considered a crime. These days, adultery drives popular culture and entertainment, and it fuels the breakup of countless marital unions. But the important point here is that the sexual revolution could never have gained the type of traction it has in the culture if adultery had continued to be understood as a great evil to be avoided and a sin to be sanctioned.

But in more recent years, the issue of adultery has become awkward simply because when people are not getting married, adultery is impossible. So, even as the vast majority of Americans at least say they oppose adultery and believe it to be wrong, it has become largely meaningless moral sentiment when marriage is removed from the equation.[9] Where there is no marriage, there can be no adultery—and that is exactly the point. Adultery disappears when marriage disappears, and the disappearance of marriage means that the notion of "extramarital sex" is losing any moral cogency.

Ultimately, seen in tandem, the contraceptive revolution, the arrival of no-fault divorce, the arrival of advanced reproductive technologies, and the social acceptance of extramarital sex and cohabitation are all evidence of the success of the sexual revolution and elements that have fueled the expansion of that revolution into terrain that the early sexual revolutionaries could never have imagined.

"A Massive Change in One Generation . . ."

The factors we have discussed with relation to marriage and the moral crisis of our age are affirmed in very powerful words by Tom W. Smith, director of the General Social Survey of the National Opinion Research Center at the University of Chicago, one of the nation's preeminent social science institutions. Smith cuts right to the heart of the matter, noting, "What we've seen is a massive change in one generation, a change that is so great that the majority of parents of young children today were raised in a different type of family than they live in today."[10] There we see the moral revolution reduced to a single sentence. At no other time in human history is it conceivable that the parents of young children would be living in families so radically different from the families they had known as young children. This rapid pace of moral and social change has led some observers to wonder if human beings are actually capable of absorbing this level of change in any healthy way. There is abundant evidence to believe that the answer to that question is no.

Heterosexuals did a very good job of undermining marriage before the culture forces began advocating for the normalization of same-sex relationships and the legalization of same-sex marriage. The marriage crisis is a moral crisis that did not start with same-sex marriage, nor will it end there. The logic of same-sex marriage cannot end with same-sex marriage. Once marriage can mean anything other than a heterosexual union, it can and must eventually mean everything—from polygamy to any number of other deviations from traditional marriage. It is just a matter of time and the progressive weakening of moral resolve.

This has all been made possible by a breakdown in the moral immune system of human society—and this breakdown was no accident. Immunologists explain that one of the wonders of human life is the fact that each of us receives from our mother an amazing array of defenses within our immune system. Throughout time, we develop further immunities to disease, or we grow sick and vulnerable. A severely compromised immune system leads to chronic disease, constant vulnerability, and potential death. If this is true for an individual, it is also true of a society or civilization.

Western civilization has forfeited its immunity against the breakdown of marriage, the family, and the integrity of human sexuality. We can point to others who have been the prophets and agents of this self-injury, but we must recognize that we have all contributed to it, insofar as we have embraced essentially modern understandings of love, romance, liberty, personal autonomy, obligation, and authority. And the separation of the conjugal union and openness to the gift of children has further undermined both our conscience and our credibility in the defense of marriage. We separated sex from marriage and marriage from reproduction. We sowed the seeds of the current confusion. At the very least, we did not address this confusion with sufficient moral clarity and credibility. To make matters infinitely worse, the failure of Christian churches to address these issues honestly and forcefully with the full weight of Christian conviction has created, in the eyes of many, an insurmountable challenge to evangelical credibility on the issue of homosexuality and same-sex marriage.

It is profoundly true that the sexual revolution did not begin with same-sex marriage. The sexual revolution began when a significant number of people in modern society decided to liberate themselves from the inherited sexual morality that had been derived from Christianity and informed the cultural consensus throughout human history. That was a decision largely made by heterosexuals who intended to legitimize their own sexual sin by means of a new moral argument. There were sexual revolutionaries advocating and hoping for the normalization of homosexuality from the beginning, but these were voices far outside the mainstream. Today's movement toward the total acceptance of homosexual behavior and relationships was only made possible because some heterosexuals first did their best to undermine marriage.

3

FROM VICE TO VIRTUE: HOW DID THE
HOMOSEXUAL MOVEMENT HAPPEN?

If the vast shift in the culture's understanding of the morality of homosexuality represents the great moral revolution of our time, then we must ask the unavoidable question: How did this happen? The question grows in intensity when we recognize just how quickly this revolution has taken place. Discovering *how* this happened is essential for Christians who are trying to live faithfully on the other side of this moral revolution.

Recent election cycles in American history provide a telling example of the great moral shift toward the normalization of homosexuality and same-sex relationships. Political commentator Kevin Phillips pointed out that in the 2004 U.S. presidential election no fewer than eleven states held referendums to ban gay marriage. Those bans, whether by referendum for legislation or constitutional amendment, were supported by vast majorities of the voters in each of the eleven states. The percentages ranged from 86 percent in Mississippi, 77 percent in Georgia, 76 percent in Oklahoma, 75 percent in Kentucky and Arkansas, down to 66 percent in Utah and Montana.[1] Phillips saw these votes as evidence of a looming Christian theocracy. In retrospect, the 2004 votes were the last gasp of the defense of marriage in a culture trending secular, not theocratic.

Compare 2004 to the 2012 U.S. presidential election. In that election cycle, four states considered measures that would have defined marriage, in one way or another, as exclusively the union of a man and a woman or, on the other hand, would have authorized the legalization of same-sex marriage. To put the matter plainly, in 2004 not one state out of the eleven in play failed to pass a defense of traditional marriage by a vast margin. Just eight years later, voters had reversed course. In 2012 not one effort to define marriage as the exclusive union of a man and a woman succeeded. And as most pundits affirmed, this trend would not be reversed.

I consider the political dimension simply to make the point that we can measure, even in terms of electoral votes, the remarkable speed of this revolution in morality. Furthermore, polling demonstrated that as recently as 2008 the majority of Americans were ready to affirm that they believed homosexual behavior to be immoral and homosexual relationships to be unworthy of legal recognition of marriage.[2] By early 2014, however, numerous polls indicated a vast shift in the American population on this issue.[3] These polls show a majority of Americans, though not an overwhelming majority, now support the legalization of same-sex marriage. An even larger majority indicated that they had no negative moral judgment upon same-sex relationships or homosexual behaviors. The most interesting aspect of the polling comes down to the fact that many of the people who were on one side of the equation in 2008, and quite ready to tell pollsters so, are now ready to be counted on the other side of the moral revolution.[4]

The momentum of this revolution is so massive that Americans who have any contact with popular culture are very aware of the narrative that policy makers and the creators of culture and moral judgment in this society are determined to write: only those affirming the normalization of all same-sex behaviors and relationships are "on the right side of history"—an audacious claim given that the homosexual movement is, in the grand scheme of history, so very young.

But this also demonstrates the fact that this movement has succeeded even far beyond the dreams of those who first framed its arguments. When the secular elites tell conservative Christians that we must change our convictions and moral judgments on the issue of homosexuality or be found "on the wrong side of history," they are stating what they truly and emphatically believe. They are certain—quite certain—that those who hold to a traditional understanding of sexual morality will be repudiated by history, and left behind by the society now taking a new shape around us.

To all these considerations, add the fact that generational change is clearly working in favor of this moral revolution. Poll after poll demonstrates that younger Americans, especially those now defined sociologically as "millennials," overwhelmingly support the new sexual ethic. As we will see, the millennials, the largest generation in American history, represent an enormous challenge to the traditional understanding of marriage and sexuality—and an even larger challenge for faithful Christian witness. So, just as the baby boomer generation dominated American public life for the last forty years, the territory ahead of us will be dominated by the millennials. Their moral judgment on homosexuality will almost certainly be the dominant American moral judgment for the foreseeable future.

The Moral Revolution: An Organized Strategy?

Moral traditionalists cannot help but ask whether or not this is all the result of an organized strategy. Did a small cadre of homosexual activists come together to hatch a revolution that would one day transform every dimension of American public life?

That kind of question is inevitable, but it is also complicated. The reality is that there was such a plot and, out of a very small group of devoted activists, a strategy did emerge—a strategy that has been overwhelmingly successful. But even as we turn to consider that strategy, we must remember that the sexual revolution was only possible because vast moral, intellectual, and cultural changes were already underway, making society ready for revolution even as a large majority of Americans held a negative judgment on homosexuality.

After the Ball: The Gay Rights Strategy

On May 22, 1977, just a few days short of my graduation from high school, I, along with several others from my church in South Florida, went to an unprecedented event at the Miami Beach Convention Center. A few months earlier, the Miami-Dade government had passed one of the nation's first gay rights ordinances. In response to this, a large group of conservative Christians and moral allies joined together in an effort to force the Miami-Dade commission to reverse its course.

I can still vividly remember the event in the convention center. The speaker of the evening was Dr. Jerry Falwell—a figure who, at that time, was known to only a few Americans outside of Virginia. Falwell addressed what he defined as the "gay agenda." These days, many people dismiss that type of language as both conspiratorial and historically incorrect. But Falwell was right. There was an agenda and there were activists behind it. Furthermore, the agenda was rather well known because the activists publicly spoke and wrote of it.

A decade later in 1989, I purchased a new book entitled *After the Ball: How America Will Conquer Its Fear & Hatred of Gays in the 90's* by Marshall Kirk and Hunter Madsen. I did not know it at the time but this book held the quintessential strategy for what became the gay rights revolution. As I read their manifesto for moral revolution, I was struck by two simultaneous realizations. The first was the heartbreaking realization that Kirk and Madsen had devised a strategy that would, quite unabashedly, turn Western civilization on its head. My second realization was even more troubling—their plan for revolution was going to work.

In *After the Ball*, Kirk and Madsen set out a program that, in retrospect, was likely even more successful than they had dreamed, largely because it focused on changing the culture, rather than just changing the laws—as in the case of the 1969 "Stonewall riots," a series of violent demonstrations on the part of the gay community in New York opposing laws against public expression of homosexuality after the police raided a gay bar. Kirk and Madsen had a far more ambitious plan. They demanded more than mere legal recognition. They demanded that American society embrace homosexuality as a normal sexual experience and view same-sex relationships on par with heterosexual marriage.

In order to get there, the authors described taking advantage of the AIDS crisis as what they called "the insurmountable opportunity." In their own words, "As cynical as it may seem, AIDS gives us a chance, however brief, to establish ourselves as a victimized minority legitimately deserving of America's special protection and care."[5] As we can now see in retrospect, the horrifying tragedy of AIDS provided a major catalyst for moving American society to reconsider its moral principles. The devastating carnage of AIDS created an opportunity that allowed for an emotional and political realignment of American morality.

Kirk and Madsen's plan also called for very concrete actions. For example, they set their attention on a pervasive and powerful public relations strategy. They criticized former efforts to normalize homosexuality as driven by homosexuals who fit the stereotypical expectations of heterosexual Americans. Their advice to activists was quite specific: "When we say *talk* about homosexuality, we mean just that. In the early stages of the campaign, the public should not be shocked and repelled by premature exposure to homo*sexual* behavior itself. Instead, the imagery of sex per se should be downplayed, and the issue of gay rights reduced, as far as possible, to an abstract social question."[6]

Kirk and Madsen also called for reaching out to liberal churches who would become key cultural allies. As many activists have recognized, the only way specifically religious arguments could be countered in the public square was to have persons who appeared as religious "experts" answering the arguments. These defeater arguments required, in their words, "publicizing support by moderate churches and raising serious theological objections to conservative biblical teachings."[7]

In one of the most successful aspects of their strategy, Kirk and Madsen petitioned the movement to "portray gays as victims, not as aggressive challengers."[8] Their advice to their own movement was incredibly specific, if not troubling. For example, they advised, "It cannot go without saying, incidentally, that groups on the farthest margins of acceptability, such as NAMBLA [North American Man/Boy Love Association—an organization affirming pedophilia], must play no part at all in such a campaign. Suspected child molesters will never look like victims."[9]

Similarly, the two argued, "For all practical purposes, gays should be considered to have been *born gay*—even though sexual orientation, for most humans, seems to be the product of a complex interaction between innate predispositions and environmental factors during childhood and early adolescence."[10] In stark contrast to the movement supporting legal abortion, Kirk and Madsen argued powerfully against any space for choice when it comes to sexual orientation: "To suggest in public that homosexuality might be *chosen* is to open the can of worms labeled 'moral choice and sin' and give the religious intransigents a stick to beat us with."[11]

In keeping with the public relations strategy, the activists promoted a strategy that would make gays look good and make "victimizers" look bad. Specifically, they called for attention to figures who could be vilified in order to further their purposes. In their words:

For example, for several seconds an unctuous, beady-eyed Southern preacher is shown pounding the pulpit in rage against "those perverted, abominable creatures." While his tirade continues over the soundtrack, the picture switches to heart-rending photos of badly beaten persons, or of gays who look decent, harmless, and likable; and then we cut back to the poisonous face of the preacher. The contrast speaks for itself. The effect is devastating.[12]

Again, the most amazing aspect of this strategy is its overwhelming success. If anything, the momentum gained by the effort to normalize same-sex relationships during the last two decades has exceeded even the wildest aspirations of these early activists.

Specific, Coordinated Strategies: Overcoming the Stigma of Being "Crazy, Sinful, Criminal, and Subversive"

While Kirk and Madsen provided the homosexual movement with marching orders, the actual outworking of the progress of the homosexual agenda has been documented in Linda Hirshman's *Victory: The Triumphant Gay Revolution*. As she argued, the public acceptance of homosexuality had to overcome what she called the "four horsemen" of moral judgment. Those arguing for the normalization of homosexuality and same-sex relationships had to overcome the pervasive judgment in American society a generation ago that homosexuals were "Crazy, Sinful, Criminal, and Subversive."[13] These four words point to the reality that the vast majority of Americans, including the intellectual elites and professionals, held a negative view of homosexuality even as recently as thirty years ago. They also are another reminder of the scale and scope of the sexual revolution's success.

Overcoming "Crazy"

Hirshman noted that until the early 1970s both the American Psychiatric Association and the American Psychological Association held that same-sex attraction was a form of mental illness. That position held sway in the psychiatric and psychological associations until—in one meeting—the American Psychiatric Association reversed its judgment.

How did such a dramatic change of opinion come about in these professional associations? Hirshman explained that a focus group of homosexual activists was established to force the American Psychiatric Association to reverse its standing on the issue. This group concentrated on one specific committee of the American Psychiatric Association known as the "Nomenclature Committee," which defined the language of their discipline used in the authoritative manual of the psychiatric profession, the *Diagnostic and Statistical Manual* or DSM for short.

Historian David Eisenbach explained in his 2006 book, *Gay Power: An American Revolution*, that the activists within the American Psychiatric Association and other allies in the homosexual movement used the tactic known as the "zap" to shut down any meeting, conference, or assembly they deemed hostile to their cause. As Eisenbach recounted, "just as political candidates were forced to embrace gay rights after having their fundraisers and offices disrupted; psychiatrists were also vulnerable to the power of the zap when it was turned on their conferences."[14]

Eisenbach also showed that the activists focused their attention on psychiatrist Robert Spitzer, the head of the nomenclature committee. Spitzer eventually settled on a way to meet the demands of gay activists, while placating some psychiatrists who were afraid of losing business if homosexuality were normalized. Spitzer proposed a new policy that would reverse the long-standing judgment of the APA and declare homosexuality to be, in itself, in no way a psychiatric problem.

At the same time, Spitzer came up with a new category known as "sexual orientation disturbance." This category allowed credentialed psychiatrists to treat persons who had a same-sex orientation but were uncomfortable with it. Eisenbach got to the heart of the issue when he wrote, "The demise of the sickness model is a monumental event in the history of the gay rights movement."[15]

Interestingly, the "zap" approach continues even now, shutting down any moral discussion on homosexuality and homosexual relationships within the context of the American Psychiatric Association. In 2008, I was invited by the American Psychiatric Association to speak on a panel in Washington, DC, related to Christian understandings of homosexuality. Upon arriving at the conference, I found that the session had been canceled due to the demands of homosexual psychiatrists and their allies within the APA. Oddly enough, the conveners of the session were themselves prominent homosexual advocates. Yet that was not enough for those who were committed to shut down any discussion about same-sex relationships and behaviors as being, in any way, a moral or psychiatric concern.

As Hirshman made quite clear, the social acceptance of homosexuality could not have happened if psychiatrists and psychologists, the high priests of the therapeutic empire, were committed to labeling homosexuality a disease. At this crucial turning point, due to the concerted and strategic efforts of homosexual activists, one of the preeminent intellectual forces in American public life—the therapeutic profession—functions as a reliable ally for the normalization of homosexuality.

In fact, the efforts of the activists have been so successful they have not only undone the original psychiatric judgment on homosexuality, but in some ways they have completely reversed the nation's moral judgments. At least in American popular culture, to consider homosexuality to be morally suspect, in any way, or a form of mental illness is culturally dismissed. "Homophobia" is now the new mental illness and moral deficiency, while homosexuality is accepted as the new normal.

Overcoming "Sinful"

Hirshman's second category, "sinful," reflects the fact that at the midpoint of the twentieth century cultural Christianity and its moral judgments were dominant in American culture. The period after World War II saw American churches and denominations explode with new members and a burgeoning cultural influence. In the 1950s and '60s, the success of any major social movement was inconceivable if it confronted the combined opposition of America's churches.

As Hirshman noted, however, some churches and denominations, along with their clergy and theologians, were ready to join the sexual revolution. At the very least, they wanted to claim that Christianity offered a mixed verdict on the issue of homosexuality—a critical development for the sexual revolutionaries. The normalization of same-sex relationships and behaviors could not have happened without a significant group of liberal Bible scholars, theologians, and religious leaders who were willing to declare that the church's position on the sinfulness of homosexuality—a position that had existed for millennia—was in error and needed a major overhaul.

Evangelical Christians should not have been shocked by this development, since theological liberalism had progressively redefined and revised the Christian faith for the better part of a century. In the same manner set by their European colleagues, the liberals populating prominent American pulpits in the early twentieth century offered a deficient version of Christianity that was accommodated to the increasingly secular worldview of the dominant culture. Accordingly, there were plenty of theologians and church leaders ready to dispense with miracles, claims of divine revelation, and assertions of church authority in favor of a liberalized Christianity that was perfectly in tune with the worldview of the secular elites.

By the time the homosexual movement was ready for its season of most active influence, the doctrinal defenses of mainline Protestant denominations were already failing. To a greater or lesser degree, theological liberalism advanced so effectively that mainline Protestants were unable to fend off its radical revision of Christian morality. As Hirshman pointed out, the overwhelming victory of the homosexual movement in the last several decades could not have happened had it not been aided and abetted by liberal religious leaders, theologians, and church officials who were ready to declare that they had "evolved" on the question of homosexuality and were ready to lead the church in a bold, new direction.[16]

This leaves conservative Christians with a significant intellectual problem: How is it that American society was so pervasively influenced by moral revolutionaries if most of the citizens who made up that society claimed to be Christians of some sort and, in particular, evangelical Christians?

At this point, we must respond with the sobering reality that America has never been nearly as Christian as many conservative Christians have claimed. The "Christianity" held by many Americans has largely lacked the serious intellectual content needed to offer any meaningful defense against the moral revolution. Far too many evangelicals held to what they rightly believed was a biblical "position" on matters of sexual morality while lacking the comprehensive biblical worldview that would have provided the intellectual sustenance for their position.

Devoid of a Christian worldview and underfed by an absence of clear biblical teaching and preaching, millions of American evangelicals moved to their own process of moral transformation on the question of homosexuality. Lacking a clear biblical argument, many began loosening their grip on the immorality of homosexual behavior. They began moving from a clear and committed biblical position to a posture of quiet toleration to an eventual—and inevitable—acceptance of homosexuality and same-sex relationships. When you combine this theological trajectory with the coming demographic dominance of the millennial generation, the challenge today's American evangelicals are facing begins to take shape.

In the main, liberal Protestant denominations have moved away from biblical teachings on human sexuality to the acceptance of same-sex relationships, the affirmation of openly homosexual clergy, and, more recently, the authorization of clergy to perform same-sex marriages. This trajectory can be traced over and over again in denominations such as the Episcopal Church, the Disciples of Christ, the United Church of Christ, the Presbyterian Church USA, and the Evangelical Lutheran Church of America. Each of these denominations, in their own way and on their own timetable, has made headlines and nationwide news by moving progressively to the left on these issues.

Furthermore, just as the majority of mainline Protestant denominations eventually capitulated to the moral revolution, some sectors of American evangelicalism were weakening in resolve and conviction on these questions. Some self-identified evangelicals are calling for a reconsideration of the Bible's teachings on homosexuality and the church's understanding of sexual morality.

One of the most prominent voices in that discussion is Brian McLaren, for many years a pastor in Maryland. McLaren argues for the total reconceptualization of the Christian faith and also speaks about his "evolution" on the question of homosexuality and same-sex marriage. His 2010 book, *A New Kind of Christianity*, makes the totality of his revisionist model of Christianity abundantly clear. In essence, he is simply repeating the same arguments made by Protestant liberals in the late nineteenth century and throughout the twentieth century.

Without any hesitation, McLaren calls for putting aside the entire theological trajectory of Protestantism since the Reformation and suggests that the church's understanding of the Bible and the gospel throughout history has been fundamentally wrong. In the face of the modern age, he appropriates writer Phyllis Tickle's suggestion that the Christian faith hold a "rummage sale" every five hundred years or so.[17] In this "rummage sale," the Christian church gets rid of doctrines it no longer needs—or, to be more blunt, doctrines and moral convictions that are now an embarrassment in the eyes of the secular culture.

McLaren also argues that the Bible should be understood as a human book—a "community library" rather than a "legal constitution." By describing the Bible as a community library, McLaren indicates that we should not seek any kind of internal consistency in the Bible. Instead, our approach to Scripture should be to find whatever might be helpful to us, as we might in any other random assortment of books.

These theological commitments allow McLaren to neutralize the moral teachings of the Christian church and speak about homosexuality, not as an issue of right or wrong, but as an issue of inclusion. In his words, "The question is complexified from 'Is homosexuality right or wrong?' to 'How should gay and straight people understand and treat one another in God's kingdom?'"[18]

In 2006, McLaren suggested a "five-year moratorium on making pronouncements" on homosexuality.[19] He called for a process of quiet conversation in which evangelicals would remain silent about the sinfulness of homosexuality in order to engage in "prayerful Christian dialogue," in which each party would be "listening respectfully, disagreeing agreeably."[20] Of course, what this "moratorium" represented was a colossal failure of pastoral responsibility. To put the matter bluntly, there is no way a minister of the gospel can look at two young men in his office who are asking for advice about their same-sex relationship with each other and tell them, with any sense of Christian responsibility, that he is committed to a moratorium on the question and that they should come back for counsel in five years.

McLaren's moratorium evidently ended sometime before September 23, 2012, when the *New York Times* announced that he had officiated at the wedding of his son Trevor Douglas McLaren to Owen Patrick Ryan.[21] The wedding announcement indicated that Brian McLaren had led a commitment ceremony with "traditional Christian elements" before family and friends. Missing from those "traditional Christian elements" was the traditional teaching of the Christian church on both homosexuality and marriage.

As Hirshman made clear, in order for moral revolutions to work, they need the support of churches. As she explained, "They are part of the unofficial apparatus of social approval, so central to the gay revolution."[22] Without the cooperation of at least some leaders and churches within organized Christianity, it is hard to say that the homosexual movement could have proved so successful during the last several decades. As we will see in a later chapter, the question now looming before us is whether evangelical Christians will maintain a clear biblical conviction on marriage and sexual morality.

Overcoming "Criminal"

The third of Hirshman's categories, "criminal," points to the reality that some states still criminalized homosexual acts and behaviors, even as recently as 2003. Revolutions in the culture and revolutions in the law are inseparable. The courts are an indispensable battlefield to force massive structural and moral change in American society.

Walter Frank demonstrated this point brilliantly in his book *Law and the Gay Rights Story*. Frank's book follows the trajectory of major court decisions on the question of homosexual acts and relationships. As he explained, "winning hearts and minds, though important, is not a guarantee of success."[23] His point is quite simple. For the movement to gain traction in American society, arguments had to be won in the courts so that changes could be forced in the law. As in so many other contentious issues in American life, a court's verdict renders a massive sense of moral authority. In the period immediately following the *Roe v. Wade* decision in 1973, polling indicated that the majority of Americans suddenly believed a woman had a "right" to an abortion and to abortion on demand. The court's weight of moral authority led millions of Americans to adopt the moral position implied by the court's ruling.

The leaders who moved to normalize homosexuality recognized that they needed both the culture and the courts on their side if their movement was to succeed. They persuaded the public by means other than the courts, but they still used the courts to add moral authority to their movement.

A succession of cases that demonstrates the moral and legal revolution in America's highest court reveals the significant role the Supreme Court plays in the issue of homosexuality. In 1986, the Supreme Court ruled that the state of Georgia was not violating the Constitution by criminalizing sodomy. Just ten years later, the court's ruling in *Romer v. Evans* decided that no state law targeting those with a same-sex sexual orientation could be constitutional. In 2003, *Lawrence v. Texas* ruled that all laws criminalizing sodomy violated the United States Constitution. It is important to note that the legal reasoning behind the court's jurisprudence on the question of homosexuality and same-sex relationships is based, quite straightforwardly, in the Constitution's guarantee, affirmed in the *Griswold* decision on contraception, of the right to privacy and in the Fourteenth Amendment's guarantee of equal protection. Again and again, the court has returned to these two legal precedents to justify striking down laws that, in one way or another, sanctioned or criminalized same-sex acts or relationships.

The court declared in the *Lawrence v. Texas* decision, as evidenced in an opinion written by Associate Justice Anthony Kennedy, that laws criminalizing sodomy violated the Constitution because they denied those with a same-sex sexual orientation the opportunity to fulfill their own most intimate and deeply passionate form of self-expression. Responding to the logic of Justice Kennedy, Justice Antonin Scalia retorted that Kennedy's logic and the majority decision would inevitably lead to the legalization of same-sex marriage—something Kennedy and his colleagues denied.

But a decade later, in the *Windsor v. United States* ruling, a majority of justices did exactly what Scalia had predicted. In fact, 2013 was a particularly crucial step forward for homosexual activists in the legal arena. In June of that year, the US Supreme Court handed down two decisions in a single day, both of them representing milestones in the moral revolution. In the *Windsor* decision, the court struck down the Defense of Marriage Act (DOMA) that Congress had passed in 1998 after the state of Hawaii haltingly moved toward the adoption of legal same-sex marriage. DOMA declared that the federal government would recognize marriage only as the union of a man and a woman, and that no state would be forced by the commerce clause of the Constitution to legally recognize a same-sex marriage performed in any other state. The *Windsor* decision's decisive strike down of DOMA immediately led to a host of changes in policy, law, and the affairs of our entire governmental system.

Once again, Anthony Kennedy wrote the case's majority opinion. Justice Kennedy argued that the federal government's Defense of Marriage Act, overwhelmingly passed by both houses in Congress and signed into law by President Clinton in 1996, was unconstitutional because it violated the equal protection clause of the Constitution with relation to same-sex couples. Even though the court did not rule that same-sex marriage must be legal in all states, it set the stage for that to happen.

The other 2013 ruling that moved the homosexual agenda forward was the court's decision on the issue of Proposition 8. In that decision, the court ruled on a technicality in order to allow a lower court's ruling to stand. In that ruling, a district court and federal appeals court in San Francisco struck down Proposition 8, which exclusively defined marriage as the union of a man and a woman. California voters did this after their own Supreme Court legalized same-sex marriage by judicial decree.

The lawyers involved in the Proposition 8 case, David Boies and Theodore B. Olson, later explained that they had been looking for a case of this magnitude. They explained how they identified and recruited plaintiffs who had the legal standing to challenge the constitutional amendment. Their strategy included finding a couple that Americans could be drawn to as representatives of the new family. They specifically wanted a lesbian couple from the professional class with at least one child. Jo Becker, investigative reporter for the *New York Times*, recounted, "To be safe, Olson wanted six couples. That way, if one couple split, or someone died, or their opponents dug up something about the background of another that could surprise them at trial, they had a fallback."[24]

This demonstrates the brilliance of the legal strategy launched by the advocates of the moral revolution. Moreover, it reveals that the legal strategy was tied to a larger cultural revolution. At every point along the way, the approach was to use the courts as a means to extend the cultural gains already occurring in the larger society. Beyond that, the court decisions would require changes in the law and the political system so that reversing the moral revolution would become difficult, if not impossible. One need not share their agenda in order to notice the brilliance of their strategy.[25]

Overcoming "Subversive"

The last of Linda Hirshman's "four horsemen" is the perception that homosexuality is *subversive* to the moral order. The effort to normalize same-sex relationships has succeeded most when it presents homosexuals as harmless neighbors, kindhearted friends, and contributing members of a happy society. The nation's entertainment culture has provided Kirk and Madsen's strategy the space it needed to thrive. A concerted effort to present a constant parade of happy, nonthreatening homosexuals in popular culture has undercut the notion that homosexuality is subversive to a healthy society.

Ironically, some radical activists feel marginalized by the effort to present a socially acceptable portrait of homosexuals and homosexual relationships to the larger culture. Many homosexual advocates note that middle-class, white, monogamous gay men and women represent almost all of mainstream media's same-sex characters.

In any event, the effort has been stunningly successful—so successful that *USA Today*, just days after the Supreme Court handed down the 2013 legal decisions, touted Hollywood as "the best man of gay marriage."[26] Reporter Marco della Cava wrote, "The nation's pop culture machine has for decades now chipped away at a once taboo topic so as to render it utterly familiar."[27] As he went on to explain, "Whether it's the antics of two gay men in the hit ABC comedy *Modern Family* or the brazen but heartfelt sexuality on display in HBO's *Behind the Candelabra*, same-sex unions seem—at least on screen and on stage—an entrenched part of our federal union."[28] That statement succinctly captures the entertainment strategy.

An effort to normalize homosexuality and same-sex relationships has driven and been driven by Hollywood for the better part of three decades. A statement made by Dustin Lance Black, winner of a 2009 Oscar for his screenplay of the movie *Milk*, which tells the story of San Francisco politician Harvey Milk, pinpoints Hollywood's powerful role in the moral revolution: "Storytelling is the only way to dispel myths. Hollywood has had a rather important role in that. We are the world's storytellers."[29]

Once again, we need to face the fact that this is not an accident but part of a concentrated strategy. In the December 1984 issue of the gay publication *Christopher Street*, Marshall Kirk joined Erastes Pill (a pseudonym for Hunter Madsen) to write "Waging Peace: a Gay Battle Plan to Persuade Straight America." In that article, Kirk and Pill wrote:

Where we talk is important. The visual media, film and television, are plainly the most powerful image-makers in Western civilization. The average American household watches over seven hours of television daily. Those hours open up a gateway into the private world of straights, through which a Trojan horse might be passed. As far as desensitization is concerned, the medium is the message of normalcy. So far, gay Hollywood has provided our best covert weapon in the battle to desensitize the mainstream. Bit by bit over the past ten years, gay characters and gay themes have been introduced into TV programs and films. On the whole the movement has been encouraging.[30]

As veteran media analyst Michael Medved has argued, the effort to push this agenda in Hollywood has been devastatingly effective—largely because no equally concentrated and invested strategy to defend marriage is present in mainstream media. Referring to the article by Kirk and Pill, Medved observed, "Hearing the agenda outlined so brilliantly in this article, can anyone doubt that part of the problem, in what some people have called the culture war, is that one side is prepared and organized and determined, and the other side is just gradually beginning to wake up?"[31]

Charting a Revolution

Intellectual honesty requires us to recognize that there was a determined group of activists who were pushing a "gay agenda." The stunning rate of their success in the field of psychiatry, popular culture, and the courts shows us that so much more was going on beneath the surface. A new set of moral sentiments was sowing seeds for a revolution, one that would bring about the normalization of homosexuality and the legalization of same-sex marriage.

Therefore, it is wrong, as many now insist, to deny that there was ever a "gay agenda." There clearly was, and the authorities who set the agenda are easy to find, as is the substance of their strategy. Moreover, it is wrong to suggest that a small band of revolutionaries are always responsible for the seismic revolution that is now taking place all around us. The movement to normalize homosexuality became a cultural and moral possibility because the American people, more secular in their thinking and more modern in their moral analysis than they may have appeared, were ready for such a revolution.

4

THE IMPOSSIBLE POSSIBILITY
OF SAME-SEX MARRIAGE

The legalization of same-sex marriage represents the leading front and the most significant structural demand of the movement to normalize homosexuality. As the philosopher Jürgen Habermas has argued, one of the main operations of society is to fulfill the function of legitimizing and delegitimizing beliefs, principles, doctrines, and practices. As in every previous human society, marriage remains the central legitimizing institution of human life. For that reason, those who are seeking to normalize same-sex relationships and same-sex acts *must* seek the recognition, credibility, privileges, and respect that marriage has historically and universally offered.

At the same time, we must recognize that marriage is simultaneously the most public and private of institutions. Even as sexual revolutionaries have used the legalization of same-sex marriage as part of their strategy for the sexual liberation for the culture at large, we also need to recognize that for many persons with same-sex orientation, the effort to legalize same-sex marriage is a deeply urgent and personal quest.

For those who understand marriage to be the lifetime union of a man and a woman on the basis of Scripture, same-sex marriage presents a situation of daunting challenge. The reason for that is quite simple: our convictions about the nature of marriage preclude us from recognizing the union of a man and a man or a woman and a woman as a real marriage. In the Christian understanding, same-sex marriage is actually impossible, so we cannot recognize same-sex couples as legitimately married. As a result, we find ourselves amid a growing number of jurisdictions and an increasing percentage of our own friends and neighbors who understand persons of the same gender to be married, while we do not, regardless of what a court may rule.

Personal interaction is not the only place where this is awkward. It also tests evangelical engagement with public policy, nomenclature, and linguistics. Some Christians try to resolve the issue by putting scare quotes around the term in order to indicate that it is a term of art rather than a term of fact. But this can confuse a public conversation since marriage, in a secular worldview, now includes same-sex couples. In that sense, not only is same-sex marriage *not* an impossibility, it is an actuality. But for our purposes, as we try to consider this issue in a way that is faithful to both Scripture and marriage, we must recognize same-sex marriage as an impossible possibility—it does not exist, but in some sense it does, and so we have to talk about it.

The Arrival of Same-Sex Marriage: A Complicated Story

The push for same-sex marriage, now understood to be a necessary outgrowth of the movement to normalize homosexuality, was not always in the foreground of the gay rights agenda. Indeed, a significant number of gay activists were adamantly opposed to any conception of gay marriage. In terms of their own self-description, the movement demanding the normalization of homosexuality includes both *liberationists* and *assimilationists.* Liberationists call for the liberation of human sexuality and of sexual morality from any negative judgment against same-sex acts and relationships. Moreover, they demand that conventional sexuality must be virtually, if not completely, eradicated in order to liberate humanity from the oppression of the past.

Assimilationists (also called accommodationists) argue that the homosexual movement should take on a less confrontational posture. If the liberationists were known for their 1990s chant "We're here! We're queer! Get used to it!" the assimilationists countered with the assertion, "We're here, but we're just like you." The assimilationists demanded marriage as the ultimate vehicle for acceptance into the privileged space of American respectability. The two opposing forces within the movement could scarcely have been more at odds.

Interestingly, significant thinkers and activists on both sides of this intramural debate have switched positions on these issues. For example, liberationists who had once opposed same-sex marriage, now see court battles and cultural victories related to same-sex marriage as stepping-stones toward a more radical liberationist agenda. Others, believing that the quest for legal same-sex marriage was doomed from the start, have now joined the movement since it has succeeded in both the courts and in the court of public opinion. Yet activists on both sides remain separated by a vast gulf—and that gulf is the institution of marriage.[1]

Redefining Marriage in the Modern Age: Another Step Toward an Impossible Possibility

To understand why the legalization of same-sex marriage is so important, we must first recognize that marriage has undergone massive displacement and redefinition in the modern age. In the first place, marriage has been transformed and minimized to the status of a contract. As we will see in a later chapter, the biblical understanding of marriage is based in a covenant, which means far more than a contract. A covenant comes with a moral pledge made before God and our fellow human creatures. When a man and woman marry, they pledge that they will remain faithful to each other, and only to each other, until parted by death. As we have seen already, that view of marriage has been pervasively subverted by the sexual revolution, the advent of no-fault divorce, the transience and disruptions of our modern economic landscape, and the ideological patterns of modern life.

Second, marriage has been redefined according to emotional satisfaction rather than objective status. Culture has largely redefined the notion of "companionate" marriage and instead embraced *eros* and romantic love as the sum and substance of the marital relationship. Though the biblical understanding of marriage certainly includes *eros* and romance between a husband and wife, the Bible does not define marriage as primarily rooted in companionship or erotic love. Instead, the Bible defines marriage in terms of the sanctity of a vow, the permanence of an institution, and as one of God's most gracious gifts to his human creatures, not the product of human social evolution.

Third, modern people, including far too many Christians, now define marriage according to their nation's legal standards. In other words, modern people largely assume that the government has the right to define marriage. While Christians should expect the government to respect and protect marriage, we cannot accept the notion that the nature of marriage is ultimately in the hands of government. Instead, Christians must insist that marriage is a *pre-political* institution. Government does not create marriage—it recognizes it. Likewise, the government does not establish marriage—it respects it. Failing to understand this, many people have fallen into the trap of simply assuming that marriage is whatever any government or system of laws says it is. While the law may redefine marriage in a legal sense, Christians must continue to affirm that marriage, in the eyes of God, remains the union of a man and a woman.

Heading for the Altar: The Place of Same-Sex Marriage in the Homosexual Movement

The proponents of legal same-sex marriage, especially among gay men, argue that marriage will have a "civilizing" effect on homosexual men. Professor William Eskridge of Yale Law School, a prominent advocate for same-sex marriage, argued that the legalization of same-sex marriage will move gay men from "sexual liberty" to "civilized commitment."[2] Eskridge, whose arguments on behalf of same-sex marriage have been massively influential, suggested that the task of "civilizing" homosexual men will include limiting promiscuity and outlandish sexual behaviors, as well as more fully integrating them into the larger community.

Others in the movement make similar points. For example, Andrew Sullivan is a particularly fascinating contributor to this conversation. His writings on homosexuality and same-sex marriage reveal the divided mind of the movement in a single individual. Sullivan believes that the legalization of same-sex marriage will also bring a civilizing influence upon homosexual men. Indeed, Sullivan blames many of the sexual behaviors and pathologies of homosexual men on the dominant community's refusal to grant them recognition of relationships through same-sex marriage. At the same time, Sullivan refuses to make same-sex marriage a normative expectation for homosexual men. Instead, he effectively argues that same-sex marriage would be a significant advance for homosexual men who might be described as the "marrying kind."

In the end, for Sullivan and for many others, the most essential issue is equality. Sullivan points to the centrality of equality in the homosexual movement:

Gay marriage is not a radical step; it is a profoundly humanizing, traditionalizing step. It is the first step in any resolution of the homosexual question—more important than any other institution, since it is the most central institution to the nature of the problem, which is

57

to say, the emotional and sexual bond between one human being and another. If nothing else were done at all, and gay marriage were legalized, ninety percent of the political work necessary to achieve gay and lesbian equality would have been achieved. It is ultimately the only reform that truly matters.[3]

That statement, in sum, explains why the homosexual movement coalesces around the demand for the legalization of same-sex marriage. Victory in this field will, as Sullivan estimates, represent "ninety percent of the political work necessary to achieve gay and lesbian equality."

That is why an emphatic "liberationist" like columnist Michelangelo Signorile recognizes the quest for same-sex marriage as a necessary means of accomplishing an eventual liberation *from* any traditional concept of marriage. As Signorile has written, the battle for same-sex marriage is "about keeping the religious Right from rigidly defining for all of America what family is, and from enforcing heterosexuality for everyone."[4]

Signorile argues that others in his liberationist camp should consider "the idea that something as traditional as marriage can be transformative."[5] But the quest for the "freedom to marry" is actually, according to Signorile, about transforming marriage rather than transforming the lives of homosexual men. As he stated unambiguously, "Rather than being transformed by the institution of marriage, gay men—some of whom have raised the concept of the 'open relationship' to an art form—could simply transform the institution itself, making it more sexually open, even influencing their heterosexual counterparts. And who's to say that broadening the terms of the marriage contract wouldn't strengthen the two individuals' commitment to it?"[6]

At this point we see the divided mind of the homosexual community, at least as represented by gay men, on the question of same-sex marriage. The assimilationists and the liberationists now appear to be united in the legal demand for same-sex marriage, but for fundamentally different reasons. Beyond this, even the assimilationists appear to be clear in stating their conviction that the entrance of gay couples into marriage—especially male gay couples—would inevitably transform marriage as an institution.

Natural Law and Christian Engagement in the Public Square

Efforts to oppose the legalization of same-sex marriage are now meeting a stiff wind of resistance in popular culture. As we saw in the previous chapter, as recently as 2008 a majority of Californian voters approved Proposition 8, which exclusively defined marriage as the union of a man and a woman—an intriguing result at the polls given that California is one of the union's most liberal states. The fact that Proposition 8 has now been dismissed as an outdated moral proposal demonstrates the enormous shift in the public opinion on same-sex marriage.

In the 2012 presidential election, just four years after Proposition 8, not one effort to defend and define marriage as exclusively the union of a man and a woman was successful. The momentum of same-sex marriage and the cultural headwinds of resistance fighting against defenders of traditional marriage and the natural family reveal that many of our neighbors lack the intellectual defenses they need to properly evaluate the arguments made by the marriage revisionists. They have seemingly lost a worldview we can only presume they once possessed. Most, however, have simply been nurtured by the secular age. Untutored and untaught by their churches and synagogues, many simply have little understanding on the comprehensive nature of marriage.

Until the present decade, arguments against same-sex marriage appeared to have traction because a majority of voters seemed to operate out of the moral intuition and conviction that marriage could only be the union of a man and a woman. Unfortunately, that conviction appears to have been built upon a foundation of sand, a foundation easily overcome by the waves of social pressure and popular culture.

Similarly, efforts to define marriage in scriptural terms now meet almost universal rejection in the secular public square. Christians should not be surprised that a secular culture rejects moral restrictions imposed by religious authority. Since a secular culture resists any binding theological authority, it will refuse to be bound by any moral restriction that, in the views of any given people, appear to restrict behaviors solely on a theological basis.

This, if nothing else, explains the changing fortunes of conservative Christians in the public square. It also explains why many people respond to polls by indicating that they are Christians of one sort or another. Even though the "nones" represent the fastest-growing group of Americans by religious affiliation,[7] the fact remains that if 20 percent of Americans identify as having no religious affiliation, this leaves 80 percent who do.

Serious biblical or theological examination of the worldview represented by that 80 percent, however, reveals its lack of binding authority. In terms of their moral judgments on many issues, a majority of Americans appear happy to discover the Bible agrees with their moral assumptions, but quite unhappy and unwilling to change their moral judgments when Scripture explicitly rejects them. In other words, even those who continue to identify as Christians reserve no space for moral authority—particularly the binding authority of Scripture and teachings of their church.

We need to recognize that when opinion is manufactured and shaped in the United States, it starts with the elites and then is adapted by the masses. As James Davison Hunter explained, "The deepest and most enduring forms of *cultural* change nearly always occurs from the 'top down.' In other words, the work of world-making and world-changing are, by and large, the work of elites: gatekeepers who provide creative direction and management within spheres of social life."[8]

This is particularly important when we consider the fact that the elites are far more secularized than mainstream American culture, and far more secularized than the middle class. Thus, those who oppose the legalization of same-sex marriage and want to protect and revere natural marriage find themselves speaking to a class most resistant to any argument from Scripture. Furthermore, as we shall see in a later chapter, these elites are doing their very best through legal means to eliminate the possibility of inherently religious moral arguments from having any role in the public square. For this reason, and others as well, a significant number of Christians now respond to the normalization of homosexuality and the demand for same-sex marriage by resorting to what is traditionally known as "natural law" argumentation.

The Meaning of Marriage and Natural Law

The shift in public discourse to natural law argumentation is easy to understand. If proponents of traditional marriage cannot gain cultural traction by citing Scripture, and if any claim of divine revelation is out of bounds in the public arena, then the best strategy would be to avoid arguments that make claims of special revelation and biblical authority.

While traditionally used by Roman Catholic philosophers, theologians, and ethicists, natural law theory has also recently attracted the attention of some evangelicals. Of course, all Christians should affirm the reality of the natural law because Scripture itself affirms both the natural law and the reality of natural revelation. Also called *general revelation*, natural revelation refers to the fact that God embedded the knowledge of himself and of his law in the universe. In other words, the Creator displayed his own moral character and the appropriate moral structure of the universe in creation.

One of the best natural law arguments is found in Sherif Girgis, Ryan

T. Anderson, and Robert P. George's book, *What Is Marriage? Man and Woman: A Defense*[9]—an expansion of their widely read article published in the *Harvard Journal of Law and Public Policy*. By any estimation, *What Is Marriage?* is a brilliant argument—indeed a tour de force.

Girgis, Anderson, and George argue that there are now two views of marriage in the larger society: a *conjugal* view that understands marriage as "a bodily as well as an emotional and spiritual bond, distinguished thus by its comprehensiveness," and a *revisionist* view that defines marriage as "in essence, a loving emotional bond, one distinguished by its intensity."[10] It is hard to miss the wisdom of this distinction, even as we hear both sides articulated in our own conversations about marriage and the debates we hear in the public square. If marriage is defined according to the *revisionist* view, there is no reason why it should *not* be redefined in a way that includes same-sex couples. There is simply no argument against such a proposal if marriage is, in fact, nothing more than a "loving emotional bond distinguished by intensity." On the other hand, if marriage is "a bodily as well as an emotional and spiritual bond distinguished by comprehensiveness," then marriage between two individuals of the same sex is, quite clearly, impossible.

Girgis, Anderson, and George, each of whom has made a tremendous contribution to the marriage debate and to our country's moral conversation, explain what it means for marriage to be a conjugal and comprehensive union. They point to the structure of the male and female human body as indicators of the conjugal union. They also point to the social meaning and importance of marriage as affirmed by virtually every civilization throughout human history. Thus, they warn that the subversion of marriage leads to unspeakable social ills and a diminishment in human flourishing. It is important also to recognize that they affirm the inherently exclusive and monogamous nature of the conjugal relationship. They document the extent to which the revisionists call for the redefinition of marriage in such a way that demonstrates "openness" and "flexibility." As the three authors rightly assert, those words are "euphemisms for sexual infidelity."[11]

This leads us to a very important reality that may make many evangelicals profoundly uncomfortable. "New natural law" theorists such as Robert P. George, John Finnis, and Germain Grisez all affirm that the "comprehensiveness" of the conjugal union includes the necessary function of procreation. The severing of procreation from the conjugal union by means of artificial contraception has profoundly redefined the meaning of marriage. At this point some evangelicals will complain that the new natural law theorists are simply trampling on intimate territory where they have no business going. Instead, evangelicals should admit that our own open embrace of the contraceptive revolution has led to a large amount of moral mischief and opened the door for the redefinition of marriage away from the conjugal vision and toward the revisionist model we now oppose.

If evangelicals are going to recover a comprehensive understanding of marriage and family, we must be willing to face the contraceptive question, and we must do so with theological maturity and ethical honesty. As I said previously, I do not believe that every *act* of sexual intercourse between a married couple must be equally open to the gift of children. I do believe, however, that Scripture teaches that every *marriage* must be open to the gift of children and that the default position for Christians must be the welcoming of children as a divine gift rather than resisted as a biological imposition.

In response, some advocates of same-sex marriage argue that the conjugal vision of marriage, tied necessarily to the function of procreation and the related natural law arguments, leads to the belief that heterosexual couples who cannot achieve pregnancy should not be allowed to marry. That is, of course, moral nonsense. Both Scripture and natural law affirm that the husband and the wife engage in the comprehensive conjugal nature of marriage, even when that union cannot be completely fulfilled with children. Thus, a married couple in their eight-ies demonstrates the glory of God even when they are past the season of procreation. A husband and wife always testify to God's purpose for marriage no matter the season of life. Similarly, an infertile man and woman are not prevented from entering into marriage, so long as they are able and faithful to provide a picture of the conjugal union in its wholeness through their openness to the gift of children, even if they are unable to receive that gift.

Evangelicals and Natural Law Arguments

Evangelical Christians, in particular, should recognize natural law as a priceless testimony to the comprehensive grace of God, a testimony that displays his glory and pattern for human flourishing. As Paul affirmed in Romans 1, God has revealed even his invisible attributes in the things that are made (v. 20). Natural revelation explains why even those who have never heard a single word of special revelation (i.e., Scripture) have an innate knowledge of God and an internal moral consciousness. This is why the apostle Paul said that there is no one who has an excuse for failing to know and honor God (v. 21).

In this sense, Christians should understand that the very best natural law arguments for marriage help us understand what is more comprehensively revealed in Scripture. Reading the work of the natural law theorists can bring a new appreciation for how the glory of God is demonstrated in the institution of marriage. They remind us that human beings are created as male and female, and that God has given his image-bearers the entire pattern of human civilization and flourishing.

Nevertheless, the ultimate authority for knowing and affirming these truths is not the natural law, but the Holy Scriptures. This is precisely the point where evangelical Christians, who base their understanding of religious authority entirely upon the principle of *Sola Scriptura*, must affirm that Scripture alone is the final authority. As the great reformer

Martin Luther stated so emphatically, Scripture is *norma normans non normata*—the norm of norms that cannot be normed.

Still, other sources of knowledge, always considered in light of Scripture, can help us affirm and apply what Scripture teaches. This is how evangelical Christians should view the natural law. We must judge it by Scripture, but we must also allow the arguments of natural law, when consistent with Scripture, to draw us into an even deeper understanding of and appreciation for the goodness of God's gifts to us.

In a major symposium on homosexuality held more than twenty years ago, my friend and mentor, the late Carl F. H. Henry, and I were invited to address the issues of authority, natural law, and homosexuality. Dr. Henry and I agreed not to review the content of our presentations until after we had made them. After the conference concluded, we were both surprised to find that we each felt compelled to address the importance of natural law arguments and to urge evangelicals never to grow dependent upon natural law arguments at Scripture's expense. My concern, then and now, was that constant recourse to these arguments would confuse evangelical Christians about the ultimate reason why we define marriage as we do—as an act of obedience to the living God.

At this point, evangelicals should simply remember that Paul not only affirms natural law in Romans 1, but also tells us how it will fare in a fallen world. Human beings steadfastly show the ability to convince themselves that they do not know what Paul insists they actually *do* know. Human beings excel at suppressing the truth of God in unrighteousness (Rom. 1:18). In other words, human rebellion and sin is the sole and sufficient explanation for why human beings follow their own moral instincts rather than submit to natural law.

If nothing else, the challenge of arguing *against* same-sex marriage should help Christians come to a deeper understanding of the arguments *for* marriage as revealed in Scripture—the faithful, monogamous, lifetime union of one man and one woman in all its glorious comprehensiveness.

But that argument also underlines the fact that same-sex marriage is, according to both Scripture and Christian tradition, an impossibility. According to some governments and courts, same-sex marriage is now an actuality. Today's Christian can only view this paradox with a sense of both concern and amazement.

5

THE TRANSGENDER REVOLUTION

Today's generation often encounters material that no previous generation could possibly have comprehended. Consider a recent opinion column written by Jennifer Finney Boylan in the *New York Times* entitled "I Had a Boyhood, Once." Writing about her three sons, she reflected on boyhood in summer and "what it means to be a boy in this country, and how boyhood has changed over time." About halfway through the article, Boylan surprised the reader with a shocking revelation: "I had summers like that, too, in the 1960s, and although I became a woman in adulthood and struggled with the gender business until then, it's nevertheless true that I had a boyhood, and that many moments in it were pretty blissful."[1] No previous generation could have made any sense of that statement. Nevertheless, her opinion column announces a monumental reality we cannot ignore: the transgender revolution has arrived.

The Transgender Revolution

A recent cover story in *Time* marked a major milestone in the transgender revolution. As the story's author, Katy Steinmetz, reported nearly a year removed from the Supreme Court's legalization of same-sex marriage, "Another civil rights movement is poised to challenge long-held cultural norms and beliefs. Transgender people . . . are emerging from the margins to fight for an equal place in society.[2]

According to Steinmetz, the transgender revolution is far from where it wants to be, but the general tone of the article and the symbolic value of a cover story for *Time* indicate that a significant cultural moment for the transgender revolution has already arrived.

As for the roadblocks this revolution faces, Steinmetz believes the biggest is the preestablished and binary definition of gender out of which people in this world operate. Such a definition of gender is not a recent development, of course. That binary understanding of human beings as male and female has been central to the human experience and our self-understanding throughout human history. The ability to "transform" gender and have "gender reassignment surgery" is so new that it was not even considered a prominent part of the gay rights movement when it emerged in the 1960s.

Today, the transgender revolution is achieving the forward momentum its activists have been seeking. The *Time* cover story fully intended to authoritatively introduce transgendered issues to the American middle class. Steinmetz did her best to show middle-class America why the transgender revolution has arrived and why it should be welcomed.

Steinmetz made her position clear when she told Americans the way they should understand the distinction between sex and gender, and sexual preferences. In her words, "Sexual preferences, meanwhile, are a separate matter altogether. There is no concrete correlation between a person's gender identity and sexual interests; a heterosexual woman, for instance, might start living as a man and still be attracted to men. One oft-cited explanation is that sexual orientation determines who you want to go to bed with and gender identity determines what you want to go to bed as."[3]

That paragraph turns an entire civilization upside down. Arguing that we should draw a clear distinction between who an individual wants to go to bed *with* and who an individual wants to go to bed *as* requires the dismantling of an entire thought structure and worldview.

This is why the transgender revolution, even more than the movement for gay liberation, undermines the most basic structures of society. As much as the gay liberation movement rejects traditional sexual morality, the authoritative teaching of historic Christianity, and the moral sanctions of virtually every civilization, it does not go so far as to reject gender distinctions or biological sex. To the contrary, the psychiatric category of "inversion," used by physicians decades ago to explain homosexuality, suggested that an exaggerated sense of gender rooted in biological sex caused homosexual orientation.

The transgender revolution, however, undermines any understanding of human identity based in the Christian tradition, the trajectory of Western civilization, and the worldview that has shaped today's world. In some European countries, preschools now prohibit the use of gendered pronouns. Similar prohibitions are being attempted in North America, most notably in Vancouver, British Columbia. Eradicating gendered pronouns and terms such as "girl" and "boy" represents the denial of Scripture's definition of our humanity. This is why the transgender revolution represents a challenge we cannot avoid.

Moreover, the transgender revolution represents one of the most difficult pastoral challenges this generation of Christians will face. Churches include individuals struggling with gender confusion just as they include individuals struggling with same-sex attraction. This kind of confusion concerns the very core of our being and cannot be pushed to the periphery of our consciousness. Our gender identity is fundamental to our self-knowledge. A biblical response to the transgender revolution will require the church to develop new skills of compassion and understanding as we encounter persons, both inside and outside our congregations, who are struggling.

The movement's own historians recognize the newness of the transgender revolution. Many historians point to the 1990s as the emergence of significant momentum in the transgender movement.[4] Yet even then it seemed to more Americans like a radical movement on the periphery of the culture.

The transgender revolution is so new on the scene that most Americans are not even certain how to talk about it. In her *Time* article, Steinmetz did her best to set the record straight, distinguishing between transgender, transvestite, and transsexual. The pioneers of the transgender revolution were identified as transvestites, which linguistically referred mostly to clothing and "cross-dressing." Those changing their gender by totally immersing themselves in the gender opposite from their biological sex were called transsexuals. Today, a transsexual may or may not have had gender reassignment surgery or hormonal treatments, but a very clear declaration to be identified as the opposite gender has been made. Transgender means exactly what it appears to mean—moving through and beyond the category of gender as it has been defined in the past. It alone reveals the comprehensiveness of this revolution.

This raises an interesting point. The word *transgender* would be largely meaningless to an individual who died just a generation ago. In common English usage, gender was a rare category, borrowed in essence from European languages that differentiated nouns by gender. The word *sex* more commonly described males and females in the United States, which is one of the reasons the feminist movement was described as a "battle of the sexes" and not a "battle of the genders" in the 1960s.

The distinction between sex and gender is not just a matter of linguistic choice—it is essential to the worldview of the transgender movement. The movement makes a sharp distinction between *gender* with regards to an individual's self-understanding and an individual's *sex*, which refers to the biological sex determined at birth. According to the Human Rights Campaign, *gender* "refers to the socially constructed roles, behaviors, activities, and attributes that a given society considers appropriate for men and women. Gender varies between cultures and over time. There is broad variation in how individuals experience and express gender."[5] *Sex*, on the other hand, refers to "one's biological and physical attributes—external genitalia, sex chromosomes, hormones, and internal reproductive structures that are used to assign a sex at birth (female/male/intersex). Also referred to as biological sex, anatomical sex or assigned birth sex."[6]

As the definition by the Human Rights Campaign makes clear, the transgender revolution required something that the gay liberation movement, at least in its early stages, did not—the arrival of postmodernism as an intellectual movement. One of the central tenets of postmodernism is that "reality" itself is socially constructed. In other words, reality is not an objective fact or a comprehensive truth, but a set of socially constructed ideas and social systems used by people in power to restrain and oppress the less fortunate. A driving concern of postmodernism was its claim to liberate those who suffered from oppression caused by patriarchy, capitalism, or Christian civilization. Status as a recognized minority most often defined those needing liberation.

The transgender revolution would have been impossible without this postmodern development, for the idea of gender as a socially constructed reality is indispensable to the transgender worldview.[7] Transgender pioneers and theorists employed the worldview of postmodernism in an effort to capsize and deconstruct traditional notions of sex and gender, which, in their view, are inherently oppressive. The liberation project aims to push humanity past traditional notions of sex and gender— and as some activists argue, beyond the very notion of gender itself. At the same time, the implausibility of this worldview to a majority of Americans explains why most people still think in the "binary" patterns of human beings as male and female.

These matters, however, require careful thinking. Christians should *not* deny that notions of masculine and feminine are, to some degree, socially constructed. Social habits, marketing forces, personal experiences, and cultural expectations do influence our notions of masculine and feminine. But this does not mean the basic understanding of humanity as male and female is itself socially constructed. That is the central claim and intellectual thrust of the transgender movement.

As with the gay liberation movement, the transgender movement looked to liberal theologians who helped further their cause. One of the most oft-cited theological authorities in the transgender movement is Virginia Ramey Mollenkott, who, at one point in her life, identified herself as an evangelical and pioneered the Evangelical Women's Caucus.[8] Now, Mollenkott advocates the concept of "omnigender," which promises to overcome the gender conflict by denying the objective reality of gender altogether.[9] In doing so, she directly counters Scripture and the church's reading of it for the last two thousand years.

In advocating her notion of omnigender in the larger society, Mollenkott, depending on the work of Martine Rothblatt,[10] anticipates a future in which all people "would have their own unique sexuality, falling in love with another person because of their emotional response to the person's entire being, not the person's genitals."[11] Furthermore, government records such as birth certificates and driver's licenses would not record sex or gender. The new future would also guarantee an individual the right to "control and change one's own body" by means of everything from cosmetic surgery to hormonal treatments, to complete gender reassignment surgery. Bathrooms would be "unisexual" as well: "Inside, they would look like women's restrooms today: no urinals, only sit-down toilets enclosed in privacy stalls."[12] She then envisions a future in which "children would be taught to sit down to urinate, regardless of their genitals."[13] This would require "public lavatory space [to be] under automatic video surveillance."[14] The omnigender revolution would require shifting away from "binary pronouns (his/her) toward gender-inclusive wording."[15] In addition, prisons and athletic sports would no longer be divided by sex or gender. Indeed, no dimension of society would be left untouched.

Transforming the way children think of gender is actually central to the transgender movement. This is evident in Welcoming Schools, a project of the Human Rights Campaign intended to further the movement's aims in public schools. Parents of children at Janney Elementary School in Washington, DC, realized just what the Welcoming Schools project planned for their children when a teacher in the school declared himself transgender and announced that he would now be addressed as "Ms. Reuter," not "Mr. Reuter." An e-mail sent to parents by the principal of the school announced how the transition of Mr. Reuter to Ms. Reuter would be explained to the children. Parents were instructed to inform their children that gender is a socially constructed reality and that the transition of Mr. Reuter to Ms. Reuter should be welcomed as an opportunity for the school and its students to show their commitment to freedom and respect.[16]

After reciting the definitions of *gender*, *gender identity*, *sex*, *transgender*, and *gender transition* offered by the Human Rights Campaign, the principal suggested that parents should be prepared to educate their children in this worldview. Parents unwilling to present this worldview to their children were instructed to educate themselves so that they would then share the worldview and help their children understand how Mr. Reuter became Ms. Reuter.

The principal, who is married to her lesbian partner, also suggested "a wide scope of educators, experts and partners" parents could consult. A few of these suggested by the principal advocate sexual practices and lifestyles undoubtedly far outside the imagination of some of the parents. The children's indoctrination included defining "gender identity" as "how one feels inside. One's internal, deeply felt sense of being girl/woman, boy/man, somewhere in between, or outside those categories."[17] Thus, elementary school–age children are being told that they should understand gender identity not only in categories of boys and girls, but even in gender identities "somewhere in between, or outside these categories."

In response to the principal's e-mail, columnist Mary Hasson refuted, "Two millennia of philosophical, scientific, and religious perspective simply vanish in [the principal's] dogmatic presentation of gender as a social construct and gender identity as a feeling-based reality disconnected from a person's biological sex."[18]

As the public's knowledge of transgender issues began to expand in the 1990s, developments emerged that captivated Americans, even as they divided them along moral lines. Oprah Winfrey, whose television show was viewed by millions of Americans, became a major advocate for transgender issues, particularly among children. Her show featured young children who expressed a desire to transition from one gender to the other. Winfrey, joined by her studio audience, often expressed outrage at parents who were unwilling to allow their children and young teenagers to undergo gender reassignment surgery. Similarly, on both sides of the Atlantic, news agencies reported stories of parents—gender revolutionaries themselves—who declared that they were going to raise their children without reference to gender. These experiments, however, generally ended as soon as the child was able to think and communicate in gendered terms.

As it turns out, those parents discovered what virtually all parents know—children identify themselves by means of their biological sex. They even do so against the advice and instruction of the gender revolutionaries. This is why the process of introducing Mr. Reuter as Ms. Reuter at Janney Elementary School required such a comprehensive public relations and communications strategy by the administration. As Hasson pointed out, the effort was unlikely to be successful among the children, no matter how hard the educators and their "experts" tried.

By now, parents should recognize that the authorized sex education programs in many public schools reflect this ideological shift. Furthermore, the entertainment industry and producers of popular culture work hard to feature transgender storylines, characters, and themes. Yet to a considerable degree, they still cannot overcome the "binary" conceptions of male and female in which the majority of Americans still think.

Some transgender advocates recognize that the effort is not working. Even a *Time* cover story featuring a prominent transgender actor is still too revolutionary and out of bounds for millions of Americans.[19] Once again, this demonstrates that the transgender revolution is even more revolutionary than the same-sex revolution.

Furthermore, the complications are endless. A news report from Arizona indicated that an individual, who was previously featured in the media as the "pregnant man," has now obtained a divorce. Thomas Beatie, as he is now known, was born female but underwent gender reassignment surgery in 2002—yet still left the female reproductive organs intact. This became a significant issue when Beatie married a woman and had a baby by artificial insemination. In granting the divorce, the appeals court in Arizona had to reject a prior judgment by a superior court judge who ruled that Beatie was not actually married. The judge ruled the marriage was actually between two females since the "pregnant man" had given birth. Lacking any other way to express his legal reasoning, that judge simply said that the marriage "was between a female . . . and a person capable of giving birth, who later did so."[20]

Once again, we observe an entire civilization collapsing. Here we find a judge who can only explain the facts of the case before him as a woman married to "a person capable of giving birth, who later did so." In any previous generation, there would have been no confusion here. Anyone "capable of giving birth" is a woman rightly described as female. The media's fascination with a "pregnant man" indicates both the scope of the revolution and the conflict with common sense and self-identity. If the gay liberation movement gained its greatest traction when it succeeded in convincing many Americans that its aims were nonthreatening, the opposite may be the case for the transgender revolutionaries. The parents at Janney Elementary School and the neighbors of the "pregnant man" are not convinced that this is a harmless revolution, even if they say they are. The tortured language of this judge in Arizona exposes the implausibility of the transgender worldview.

The End of Gender and the Challenge of the Transgender Agenda

As we will see, the transgender revolution presents a vexing dimension to the challenge Christian churches, families, and institutions will face regarding religious liberty. Recent controversies at California Baptist University and Azusa Pacific University demonstrate this reality. In the case of Azusa Pacific University, a female professor and former chairman of the theology department announced her intention to become a man. She was shocked when the Christian university found her announcement incompatible with its moral code.[21] Just a few days later, California Baptist University in Riverside made national headlines when the school expelled a male student who had appeared in the media claiming a new identity as a young transgender woman. Given California law and the government's nondiscrimination policies, both institutions were put on the defensive.[22] Furthermore, both schools are accredited by regional agencies that have their own nondiscrimination policies. When we look at religious liberty in chapter 8, we will see that the transgender revolution poses a unique set of challenges related to admission, hiring, and housing for schools. Of course, these challenges will only escalate as the transgender revolution continues.

The reality is that there is no end to the transgender revolution; endurance is one of its central dynamics. Consider the anagram by which the organized gay liberation movement is identified. During the last twenty years, the movement identified itself as LGBT, which represented lesbians, gay men, bisexuals, and the transgendered. In more recent years, the movement has fragmented due to the limitless radical expansion of groups identifying as sexual minorities, each demanding their own agenda, liberation, and public recognition. Allan Metcalf, who writes on academic issues at the *Chronicle of Higher Education*, has argued that educators "learned that we don't have to conform to a label imposed on us by others; we get to choose our gender identity for ourselves, to decide whether gay or straight, male or female, in between—or none of the above."[23] Once again, the "in between—or none of the above" reflects the never-ending and ever-expanding nature of this moral revolution.

By combining the now generally accessible initials for recognizable sexual minority groups, Metcalf came up with the anagram "LGBTQQ2IA."[24] As he acknowledged, some gay activists have seen this anagram as cumbersome and instead opt for the anagram QUILTBAG, which stands for "Queer/Questioning, Undecided, Intersex, Lesbian, Transgender/Transsexual, Bisexual, Allied/Asexual, Gay/Genderqueer."[25] Speaking of students, Metcalf simply advised, "So young people nowadays have choices to make that they didn't face before. And it's not a once-for-all choice; they can question and redefine themselves at any time."[26] The radical nature of that statement is hard to express. The transgender revolution progresses in such a way and at such a rate that an infinite series of initials can be generated to create an anagram that young people can change as they please. An endless permutation is available to them. To no surprise, the language strains to carry the weight of such a revolution.

In a follow-up to "LGBTQQ2IA," Allan Metcalf wrote another article titled "What's Your PGP?"—an acronym that stands for "preferred gender pronoun":

It's a question we didn't have to answer in the 20th century. In fact, it's a question that didn't exist until recently. . . . Nowadays we understand that anatomy isn't destiny; it's your choice to be called lesbian, gay, bisexual, transgender, queer and questioning, intersex, asexual—or something else. That's not a misstatement. It is your choice, we have been told. We have reached the point that regardless of anatomy, you can choose your gender identity. And you can choose to change your gender identity as often as you change your clothes.[27]

From this new reality emerges a question we simply never had to ask before: What pronouns should others use in talking about you? In other words, what's your PGP? In fact, the group known as the Gay Straight Alliance for Safe Schools has put out an article entitled "What the heck is a 'PGP'?" which provides a host of options beyond the binary "he/she" or "him/her" choices.

Some people prefer that you use gender neutral or gender inclusive pronouns when talking to or about them. In English, the most commonly used singular gender neutral pronouns are **ze** (sometimes spelled **zie**) and **hir**. "Ze" is the subject pronoun and is pronounced /zee/, and "hir" is the object and possessive pronoun and is pronounced /heer/. This is how they are used: "Chris is the tallest person in class, and ze is also the fastest runner." "Tanzen is going to Hawaii over break with hir parents. I'm so jealous of hir."[28]

The use of PGP is, however, not merely a suggestion on many college campuses around the nation. Rather, administrations are now enforcing policies through school legislation on speech codes that professors, administrators, and fellow students utilize these pronouns.[29] And, of course, what happens on the American college and university campus never stays there, nor is it intended to. These speech codes will ultimately trickle down to local high schools, kindergartens, and preschools. Ultimately, they may become the only acceptable mode of discourse in the public square.

The Transgender Movement and the Church's Response

The Christian response to the transgender movement must begin with Scripture. Scripture treats what the transgender movement discards as the "binary system of gender" as part of the goodness of God's created order. Genesis 1–2 presents our embodiment as male or female as essential to our self-identity not only as humans who constitute a human family, but as individuals. Every individual is made in God's image. As Denny Burk rightly argued, "We dare not miss that God created sexual differentiation. The terms *male* and *female* are not cultural constructs. They are not social roles foisted upon mankind by the accretion of culture and tradition. *Male* and *female* designate the fundamental distinction that God has embedded in the very biology of the race."[30]

Our identity as man or woman is not the result of a biological accident. The doctor at our birth does not impose it on us. It is not foisted upon us by our society's social expectations, moral habits, and cultural meanings. Our identity as man or woman is who we are. Those born as intersex, hermaphroditic, or someone with ambiguous genitalia should never be treated as if they are less human. They remind us of two profoundly important truths. First, we are all equally made in God's image and each of us is equally able to demonstrate the glory of God in our creaturely existence, just as we are all equally accountable before God as our Creator. Second, they remind us that the consequences of Adam's sin even impact our genetic chromosomal structure. Ambiguous biological sex shows us that even our biology demonstrates our fallenness.

What differentiates the transgender movement is the intention to *change* one's gender identity from one's biological sex. In fact, claims that an individual's mental wiring is incompatible with the body now drive the movement. We increasingly hear the argument that an individual is "fixing" the body so that it will correspond with the individual's consciousness. Christians must think with great care at this point. We must look to Scripture in order to understand how to situate this moral challenge within the storyline of Scripture and in accordance with what God's Word teaches. We unflinchingly hold, therefore, that to be born male is to be male and that to be born female is to be female.

The binary system of gender is grounded in a biological reality that is not socially constructed. While admitting that in the fallen world every society accumulates socially constructed ideas about gender that are often wrong and inconsistent with Scripture (and thus to be confronted and corrected), the Christian stands obligated under scriptural authority to insist that the gender assigned by biological sex is not an accident. We affirm that biological sex is a gift of God to every individual and to the human community to which that individual belongs.

This means that Christians must confront the transgender ideology at its very foundation, while also admitting that the church has often borrowed from the culture to make assumptions and expectations about gender that are socially constructed and not biblically sustained. Furthermore, we must admit that Christians have sinned against transgender people and those struggling with such questions by simplistic explanations that do not take into account the deep spiritual and personal anguish of those who are in the struggle.

Moreover, we must understand that the argument that says the brain is wired differently than the body does not justify reason for sex reassignment surgery or the transgender option. Rather, it testifies to the brokenness of creation and the effects of human sin. It is an opportunity for the Christian to respond with the message of the gospel and with the recognition that every Christian is a broken individual seeking wholeness in the only place it can be found—in obedience to Scripture under the lordship of Christ.

All of this points to a host of difficult pastoral and congregational quandaries. In due time, extremely specific and difficult questions will arrive at the doorstep of every congregation. What do we do when an individual comes to our church who is living out a gender identity that is opposite from his or her biological sex? When should such an individual, professing Christ and repenting of sin, be baptized and welcomed within the congregation? What is the long-term expectation for how obedience and submission to Christ should be demonstrated in the life of this believer? These questions are only further complicated by surgical interventions and other factors that may enter into the pastoral situation. Some of these questions will be addressed at the end of this book, but at this point, it is sufficient to say that every congregation will face these questions—and they are likely to arrive sooner rather than later.

Christians committed to Scripture cannot accept the logic of "omni-gender" or the effort to "move beyond gender," or even the effort to blur gender lines. Faithfulness requires not only that we refuse to accept this logic, but that we challenge it with the clear teaching of Scripture. Furthermore, when we do so, we are not merely entering into a difficult and painful arena of intellectual and ideological conflict; we are entering into an arena in which eternal destinies are at stake. When we enter this arena, we are confronting principalities and powers no previous Christian generation has encountered.

If nothing else, the transgender revolution shows Christians that the gospel confronts ideologies, patterns of deception, and spiritual opposition in every generation. The fact that we fight not against flesh and blood, but against principalities and powers, is perhaps never more poignant and important than in the midst of a struggle. The transgender movement reminds us whom we are really fighting. We must remember we are fighting with a gospel that cannot fail.

Gender Reassignment Surgery in
Theological and Moral Perspective

The church must also respond to the transgender movement by rejecting both the reality and the morality of gender reassignment surgery. Though we certainly must sympathize with the personal anguish and confusion that causes any individual to seek such a drastic and surgical option, we cannot accept that a surgical procedure can actually change a man into a woman or a woman into a man. We are witnesses of a massive effort of societal self-deception on this issue. We are also witnesses to the failure of that self-deception. No one claims that the basic chromosomal structure of an individual can be changed by surgery or any other medical means. The only thing actually happening is the amputation of organs combined with cosmetic procedures that attempt to create the impression of one sex rather than the other. Added to this are hormonal treatments and other procedures that try to enhance the alignment of the body's morphology with the newly declared gender identity.

Christians cannot avoid the moral conclusion that this amounts to a mutilation of the body. The biblical worldview insists that our embodiment actually demonstrates God's love for us, his gift to us, and part of his purpose and plan for our lives. To amputate and cosmetically reform the body in this sense is an act of defiance against the Creator's purpose. Where one might claim that there is a disconnect between self-consciousness and embodiment, the Christian must tenderly and compassionately advise that it is the mental—that is, the self-consciousness and sense of personal identity—that must be conformed to the body rather than the body conformed to the individual's mistaken self-perception.

At this point, we need to note that every single one of us is afflicted by a mistaken self-perception. Our self-perception, whether on this issue or any other, must be corrected by Scripture. Furthermore, Scripture itself attests to the fact that our bodies are not accidents that happen to us, but part of God's intention for us. David's confidence that God stitched him together in his mother's womb (Ps. 139:13) biblically affirms that we are not accidents in any area of our lives. The infancy narratives of both John the Baptist and Jesus reveal that their biological sex was important before they were even born (Luke 1). As the giver of life, our Creator knows us before any other knows us. Before our mothers even know we are in the womb, we are known—as male or female—by the Creator who made us so for his glory and our good.

Interestingly, even some medical authorities now also insist that gender reassignment surgery is not only inadvisable, but wrong. Paul McHugh, former psychiatrist-in-chief at Johns Hopkins Hospital, shared that he was part of the first venture into "sex-reassignment surgery" in the United States. Under his leadership, Johns Hopkins University became the first American medical center to perform these procedures in the 1960s.

Reflecting upon this later, McHugh recalled that he and his colleagues performed a study comparing the outcomes of transgendered persons who had the surgery with those who did not. He wrote, "Most of the surgically treated patients described themselves as 'satisfied' by the results, but their subsequent psycho-social adjustments were no better than those who didn't have the surgery. And so at Hopkins we stopped doing sex-reassignment surgery, since producing a 'satisfied' but still troubled patient seemed an inadequate reason for surgically amputating normal organs."[31]

Christians recognize that the inclination of every sinful human heart is to find security and salvation in something outside of Christ. If only pills, therapy, or a surgical procedure could deal with our problems, we would not have to deal with the reality of our sin. And we would not have to confront the solitary provision for that sin in the atonement accomplished by Jesus Christ. As with the contraceptive revolution, far too many evangelicals rapidly accept the medicalization of a moral issue. We must be careful that we do not allow the transgender revolution to become an opportunity for us to fail once again. We cannot allow ourselves to mistake a medical definition for a moral and spiritual reality.

Once again, these are the types of conversations that previous generations of Christians never needed to have. But, moving forward, Christians must remember three very important points. First, the intellectual and moral heritage of the Christian tradition provides a wealth of theological reflection on the issues of gender and sexuality. We must resist facile and shallow responses to the challenges of our day by reminding ourselves of the enormous theological tradition we gladly inherit from our past. Second, we must always remember that the Scriptures are sufficient to engage these challenges (we will say more about this in chapter 7). Christians need to remember that the sufficiency of Scripture gives us a comprehensive worldview that equips us to wrestle with even the most challenging ethical dilemmas of our time. Finally, as mentioned before, the gospel provides the only true remedy for sexual brokenness. The theological and pastoral challenges we face in the transgender revolution are indeed enormous, but they are not beyond the sufficiency of Christ's cross and resurrection.

6

THE END OF MARRIAGE

"It was the best of times, it was the worst of times." This opening line from Charles Dickens's *A Tale of Two Cities* aptly describes the state of marriage in our own day. In the city of marriage—that is, the sectors of society where marriage is highly honored and respected—marriage is doing quite well. In fact, recent studies have debunked the oft-repeated assertion that half of all marriages end in divorce. A closer look at the statistics indicates that a majority of marriages actually last a lifetime. Furthermore, surveys show that the vast majority of married people describe themselves as happy, fulfilled, and unwilling to contemplate any other condition of life.[1] In the other city, however, the sexual revolutionaries have drastically subverted marriage. In that city, marriage is not honored and is largely marginalized. It is a land where sex and reproduction have been decoupled and removed from the confines of marriage. Marriage has been so dislocated in the city of the revisionists that some middle school American children now report that they have never even *seen* a wedding.

How do we explain these two cities of marriage? How is it that the most central institution of human civilization and human flourishing has been eclipsed and marginalized in the modern age? The question itself contains at least part of the answer. Modernity has not been good for marriage. Nevertheless, there are good arguments that show, at least to some extent, modernity's positive contribution to the welfare and stability of marriage. Increased levels of education, economic attainments, relative security, and the development of the modern democratic state have all contributed, in some sense, to the stability of marriage among the married. Modernity tends, even as its earliest exponents understood, however, to undermine the expectations and assumptions that situate marriage as the defining mark of adulthood, personal responsibility, parenthood, and identity.

Modernity and the End of Marriage

Karl Marx, one of the primary influencers of modernism, recognized the influence of modernism when he described it with the words "All that is solid melts into air." Modernity erases kinship structures, redefines community, establishes the individual as the most important unit of meaning, and sets loose a massive set of social changes that tend to pull the family apart rather than hold it together. In fact, Marx indicated that he saw the rise of capitalism as the enemy of the family.

One hundred fifty years later, conservative Christians can understand and sympathize with at least part of Marx's critique. The modern consumer economy has proved to be toxic for marriage and family in many ways. Modern corporations have no pangs of conscience transferring their employees coast to coast multiple times over the course of only a few years. The impact of this modern vocational reality on many American marriages and families is massive. Husbands, wives, and children are uprooted from the support structures of friendship and community, and the sustenance of long-lasting relationships. The family is continually dropped into new and unfamiliar contexts, largely due to the fickle nature of economic factors.

Before the arrival of modernity, personal identity was established in the context of relationships that were established through long-standing structures of kinship and community. People born two centuries ago realized their identity in terms of parents, extended family, and neighbors. In almost every case, these communities and kinship structures were established through years, if not decades and centuries, of continuity in one place. Henry Adams, a historian who lived late in the nineteenth century, remarked that the average boy born in the United States before 1900 was unlikely to have traveled more than fifty miles from the place of his birth. The massive transformations of the modern age changed all of that for Americans.

Not all of these transformations have represented a danger to marriage and the family, of course, and no sensible person should try to reverse the genuine gains of modernity. Nevertheless, Christians must think hard about these issues. Before we take stock of the impact of same-sex marriage, we must recognize that the modern age had already begun the process of transforming marriage.

Sociologists Brigitte and Peter Berger helped define the situation by illustrating that the modern age has made the family and marriage a "problem."[2] The Bergers note that in the modern age, marriage has been displaced from its status of near-universal respect to its current condition as a mere contractual option. In previous centuries, marriage was part of the private domain but respected in the public sphere because it was the sanctioned context for the most intimate of human relationships—starting with the conjugal relation of the husband and wife and then extending to their role as parents. British common law affirmed that "every man's house is his castle" because the government understood the public significance of marriage and respected this most private of relationships. The public sensed the responsibility to protect the sanctity of that relationship against all efforts that sought to subvert or undermine it.

In a similar way, Christopher Lasch spoke of the displacement of the family and marriage from its former place as a "haven in a heartless world" to its current status as an institution standing on tenuous ground in a society in which the state is evermore present and the forces of the modern age are battering at the family's door.[3] Lasch warned that marriage and the family are now surrounded by a host of "experts" who intend to bring their own agendas and expertise into what was once considered a private domain. These experts of the therapeutic age now inform married couples of what is expected for their mutual fulfillment. They tell husbands and wives that if their personal fulfillment is limited in any way by marriage, then there is always the opportunity, if not the responsibility, to exit the marriage for the sake of personal "authenticity."

Recognizing these observations is critical if we are to rightly understand the perilous situation marriage was in long before the arrival of the sexual revolution. One of the most troubling trends in modernist societies is "the increasing distance, if not separation, of fathers from their children."[4] The modern age has brought a massive surge in children born out of wedlock. In fact, in many of these cases, the father is not even aware of his paternity.

In the lives of most of these children, fathers are largely, if not completely, absent. Add to this the trauma inflicted upon marriage and family by divorce, and the situation is compounded for children born even to married couples. I recently sat next to a man on an airplane who explained to me that, while making two business trips, he first had to fly to a city several hundred miles away to return his children to his ex-wife so that they could attend their first day of school. I felt sympathy for the tired and frustrated man. Yet I also saw an entire civilization falling apart in his situation. It made perfect sense to him to ferry his children back and forth from homes hundreds of miles apart, and, even though he was their father, to have his children visit him rather than for him to be a constant presence in the home.

Recounting the subversion of marriage in the modern age is a matter of moral responsibility as we face the challenge of same-sex marriage in the sexual revolution. Conservative Christians far too quickly accuse the proponents of same-sex marriage of being the enemies of marriage, believing that marriage was in great shape before same-sex couples started clamoring for the legal recognition of their unions. This is intellectual dishonesty, and the record must be set straight. The previous damage to marriage can be traced to the intellectual, sexual, legal, and therapeutic subversion of marriage by *heterosexuals*.

As we saw earlier, the threats to marriage and to sexual sanity emerged with developments that long preceded today's gay rights movement. The arrival of birth control allowed for the development of the "contraceptive mentality" that largely, if not totally, severed procreation from the act of sex and the context of marriage. Reason alone reveals that a massive check on sexual promiscuity would still be in place if the birth control revolution had not arrived. But that revolution did arrive, and has been a fact of life for decades. The separation of sex and procreation effectively meant the separation of sex and marriage.

All of this was at the hands of heterosexuals who followed the moral logic of the modern age and succumbed to their own demand and desire for sexual fulfillment outside the bonds of marital fidelity. Add the divorce revolution to this scene and the picture only grows more disastrous. If birth control and abortion made every pregnancy either avoidable or tentative, the arrival of no-fault divorce made every marriage tentative. Many couples now take traditional wedding vows with their fingers crossed behind their backs. The growing use of prenuptial agreements points to the fact that many couples are now getting married only after making provision for what will happen if the marriage should end. In the modern age, the language of the marriage covenant is often merely an artifact of social etiquette. In the minds of many couples, it is a statement of aspiration rather than a commitment.

Modernity has washed away many of the structures, intellectual presuppositions, and moral commitments that made marriage secure and stable. In many respects, the real debate in America today is whether or not our society should even try to overcome our tragic and subversive experiments with marriage.

Homosexuality and the End of Marriage

This brings us to the debate of greatest intensity in our time—the normalization of homosexual relationships and the legalization of same-sex marriage. Leaders within the LGBT community were divided over the question of marriage from the start. Even as figures such as Evan Wolfson, Jonathan Rauch, Andrew Sullivan, William Eskridge, and others promoted the legalization of same-sex marriage, others in the LGBT community argued that same-sex marriage would represent regression—treason against the very premise of sexual liberation.

This division within the homosexual community over this question is demonstrated in the news whenever a gay rights parade garners media attention. In most major cities, the participants include those who want to assimilate into the larger society as married couples with children. Many lesbian and gay couples do their very best to look like Cam and Mitchell on *Modern Family*, desiring the appearance of social stability, respectability, and conventionality in their private lives. But the more radical sexual liberationists are often more visibly represented in these parades. They want nothing to do with same-sex marriage because marriage is not a goal to be achieved; it is an obstacle to overcome on the path to complete sexual liberation.

In either case, the goal is ultimately the same. One side of the LGBT movement believes that granting same-sex couples access to the institution of marriage delays the final goal of complete sexual liberation.

On the other hand, proponents of same-sex marriage see its arrival as a massive step forward on the path to sexual liberation. In any event, both sides recognize that the legalization of same-sex marriage radically redefines both marriage and family.

Gay Families and the End of Marriage

At this point, we must also consider another important issue—children. Demands for the legalization of same-sex marriage have gained significant traction as Americans have become more aware of the reality that gay men and lesbians are raising children and organizing themselves as families.

The controversy over gay families first emerged in the fight for the rights of homosexual persons to adopt children. During the last several years, most states have adjusted their laws to allow, in one way or another, homosexual couples to adopt. Furthermore, a range of adoption possibilities and foster care arrangements allow many homosexual individuals and couples to move toward adoptive parenthood.

In general, Americans have voiced a growing willingness for homosexuals to adopt children. Beyond adoption, homosexuals (as individuals or as couples) have virtually unlimited access to advanced reproductive technologies. In fact, the United States has witnessed more controversy over the legalization of same-sex marriage than the question of parenthood.

The impact of homosexual parenting in the lives of children is a matter of fierce cultural debate. A study undertaken by sociologist Mark Regnerus of the University of Texas demonstrated negative impacts among children being raised in the context of a same-sex home.[5] Regnerus was ruthlessly attacked by advocates of same-sex marriage for his study. Indeed, in secular circles, it is now largely taken for granted that any evidence of this sort ought to be simply dismissed out of hand as intolerant and homophobic—as was the case during the Proposition 8 trial at the Federal District Court in California.

The defenders of traditional marriage and the natural family are at an emotional disadvantage on this issue since it is often presented to the public in terms of a strict dichotomy: children will either be nurtured and cared for by same-sex couples or they will be abandoned to the foster care system—or worse. This presents a unique challenge to conservative Christians and other defenders of traditional marriage. Regretfully, many Christians have too quickly provided trite ethical responses to what is, in truth, a serious moral issue. But the future of the church cannot depend on simplistic, unrealistic, and theologically anemic assertions that have characterized many Christians in the past on this issue.

The Christian moral tradition, sustained by centuries of serious intellectual effort, reminds us that the rescue of a child is always a virtuous act. The question now is how Christians should think about same-sex couples "rescuing" a child from the foster system or a life without family. The answer is not simple and requires careful thinking.

At present, it appears that mainstream American society has decided that male and female homosexual couples who demonstrate stability and social commitment qualify as adoptive parents. This puts the defenders of marriage and the natural family in an awkward position. Yet we must always be ready to state publicly our gladness that children are cared for, even as we assert the deficiencies of the home in which these adopted children find greater security, love, nurture, and comfort.

This will require Christians to form more mature and theologically sustainable arguments than we have brought to the public square in the past. Frankly, we will make fools of ourselves if we suggest that it would be better for children to be consigned to the anonymous social welfare system, with little hope of eventual rescue, than to be adopted by homosexual parents who deeply desire to invest themselves in the care and nurturing of children.

Christians must affirm that it is not wrong to see a child happy, and we must applaud when a child is being rescued from danger and a context of want. And, of course, we must recognize that it is not wrong to hope that a child adopted by gay parents grows up in great happiness and with the potential for flourishing. That is the right moral instinct.

Yet we must also assert that it is wrong to look at our current situation and not voice opposition to the brokenness that is present and will always be present in the fiction of gay marriage. While the world embraces homosexual families as healthy contexts for children and even presents them as such through the media, Christians must remember that the true context for human flourishing is the natural family, centered in the conjugal union of husband and wife.

Christians must also remember that we have faced a similar situation in divorce. In the aftermath of many divorces, many Christians concerned for the well-being of the children seemed to argue that if a marriage could not be restored, then the brokenness simply could not be overcome. But divorce is not the end of the story, nor is it the limit of our moral responsibility. Our responsibility in the wake of a divorce is to affirm that the context that leads to the greatest flourishing and security for children has been broken—and that the marriage covenant has been violated—even while recognizing that the children bear no responsibility for their predicament. The same is true for children who grow up with same-sex parents.

"Having Children" and the End of Marriage

All of this poses another serious issue. Previous civilizations could never have comprehended the idea of a "gay family" since gay couples cannot produce children. The advent of advanced reproductive technologies, however, has changed this basic fact. The United States has become, even by the standards of liberal and secularized Europe, the "Wild, Wild West" of reproductive technologies. We do not even have sufficient laws against human cloning or the use of clonal technologies. Christian couples often assume that as long as these advanced reproductive technologies are employed by married heterosexual couples, there is no moral complication. But there is, of course. If concern only arises when same-sex couples have access to advanced reproductive technology, Christians will be ill prepared to answer questions about these technologies in a way that is consistent, honest, and faithful.

For example, many Christians have never paused to consider the assault upon human dignity that often attends the process of in vitro fertilization (IVF). The separation of procreation from the context of the conjugal act has led to the fact that procreation, in this sense, can now be separated from sex altogether. Furthermore, the use of donor gametes, even by a married heterosexual couple, brings an alien third party into the marriage unit through the gamete donation of either sperm or egg. Add to this the now burgeoning market in surrogate mothers and the alienation grows even more extreme.

Long before we were confronted with the challenge of whether or not same-sex couples should have access to these technologies, heterosexuals were growing accustomed to an open market of sperm and eggs, the routine use of surrogate motherhood, the entrance of third parties into the marital union by means of gamete donation, and the separation of conception and procreation from the conjugal act within the covenant of marriage. Heterosexuals were redefining what it meant to "have" a child well before same-sex couples and individuals demanded access to these technologies.

It is necessary, at this point, to remind ourselves of some basic principles of Christian moral logic. One of these principles is that the more an act is alienated from its rightful context, the greater the potential there is for harm. Put plainly, this means that a heterosexual couple united in marriage, committed to the faithful insertion of every fertilized embryo within the woman's womb, and unwilling to abort or neglect any child at any stage of development is at a significantly lower moral risk than a single woman seeking to have a child by means of donor insemination, or an unmarried couple who wants to have a child through other advanced technologies. The further we alienate an act from its moral context, the greater the moral risk and the greater the opportunity for sin and sinful effect.

Thus, when we consider the issue of reproductive technologies, we must remind ourselves that their arrival makes it quite possible for a single woman to have a baby without a husband and even without an act of coitus. It is now possible for a married couple to reject an embryo that does not meet their exact specifications and to demand a designer baby instead. It is now possible for a single heterosexual man to hire a surrogate mother to bear a child, who could be brought about by means of his sperm or by some other donation of sperm and egg. All of these represent varying acts of moral responsibility that alienate the conception and birth of the child from the marital union where it should rightly be situated. The more we alienate the act of having children from the natural family and the institution of marriage, the more the picture breaks.

Now, consider the addition of same-sex couples and individuals demanding equal access to these technologies to the "Wild, Wild West" of moral responsibility. As with the case of the general subversion of marriage, gay men and lesbians are rather late to the project of dismantling parenthood, along with its rights, privileges, and responsibilities.

If nothing else, this reminds us that our responsibility to consider the moral effects of advanced reproductive technologies does not begin and end with the question of same-sex couples and their access to it. At an even more fundamental level, it reminds us that the end of marriage is now staring us in the face. Even as the entire process of "having children" is further alienated from marriage, marriage has become simply an option rather than an expectation. Once human beings were able to have sex without children and children without sex, marriage simply became a lifestyle option. Add to this the change in the Western understanding of marriage from covenant to contract and you have a sure recipe for social disaster and the subversion of marriage.

The End of Marriage: Polygamy and Beyond

Our consideration of the end of marriage is not complete without understanding that the social, moral, and legal revolutions that have accompanied the sexual liberation strategy cannot possibly stop with just granting legal marriage recognition to same-sex couples. As the defenders of traditional marriage have warned for many years, the legalization of same-sex marriage will necessarily open the door, in both logic and the law, to the recognition of polygamy and a multitude of other sexual relationships.

Some proponents of same-sex marriage have argued that this warning is nothing more than a fallacious "slippery slope" argument. But the fact is that once marriage can be redefined as something other than the monogamous union between a man and a woman, it can be defined virtually however a culture wants. Furthermore, the arguments made by same-sex couples for gay marriage are often based on personal privacy and the welfare of children, which are the same arguments we can expect from polygamous and polyamorous unions as well. This is not merely a hypothetical concern; it is already a matter of current litigation.

As I mentioned earlier, in 2013 federal judges in Utah struck down that state's prohibition against same-sex marriage and, in a separate case, also invalidated that state's historic law against polygamy. The fact that this occurred in Utah is not without historical interest since the United States government *required* Utah to outlaw polygamy, then common among many Mormons, as the cost of Utah entering the union as a state. Now, the very legislation demanded by the federal government as the price of entering the union has been declared unconstitutional by a federal court on the basis of the reasoning employed in arguments for same-sex marriage and, we should note, contraception and abortion.

Thus, the accusation that defenders of traditional marriage employ slippery slope arguments simply does not stick. What is fallacious is accusing an argument of committing the slippery slope fallacy when those arguments are buttressed with an explanation of causation. As recent court cases and public conversations demonstrate, the very arguments used to support the legalization of same-sex marriage leaves the society defenseless to argue against polygamy. The causality centers on the fact that the separation of the definition of marriage from the conjugal and comprehensive union of a man and a woman removes any objective argument against the recognition of other forms of adult, consensual, nonreproductive relationships.

The exponents of same-sex marriage often counter that there are legitimate arguments against polygamy, incest, and other sexual possibilities on the basis of sociological evidence rather than mere moral judgment. The problem with this type of reasoning is evidenced by the defenders of same-sex marriage themselves, who in their own legal arguments—as in the Proposition 8 case—simply dismissed any sociological argument that was contrary to their legal goal as being without scientific merit.

This gets to one of the most troubling moral quandaries of current secular thinking on sex and relationships. For most men and women in our culture, the only moral criterion to use when assessing the morality of sexual relationships is the issue of *consent*. From a Christian perspective, consent is simply not enough to establish any kind of sane sexual morality. A graphic illustration of that truth is seen in the recent irrational conversations concerning the epidemic of rape and sexual abuse on American college campuses. There is no doubt a very real epidemic of rape and sexual assault, mostly focused against young women, on these college campuses. Yet what the prophets of the new sexual morality fail to understand is that consent simply is not enough to protect young women once all the other moral defenses are removed. The legal mechanisms used in arguments over whether or not consent has been "granted," which has led to the complicated sex codes now given to students on the average college campus during orientation, proves the irrationality of this kind of thinking. As Christians we ought to be concerned about the very real problem of sexual violence and assault. We must sympathize with the victims of those assaults and with the plight of the sexually vulnerable in all places. Yet Christians must also recognize that a society determined to make consent its solitary moral norm will not be able to protect anyone in the long run.

What we also need to recognize is that when the issues of polygamy and related sexual relationships arrive in our cultural attention, we have already passed a significant moral barrier, and the end of marriage is now clearly and undeniably in sight. We need to keep in mind what some of the advocates of same-sex marriage have claimed all along: that the legalization of same-sex marriage is a mechanism for transforming the entire institution of marriage and for redefining the family.

Furthermore, we have to consider the diminishing social disapproval toward polygamy and polyamorous relationships. The popularity of the HBO series *Big Love*, along with arguments now routinely made in academic circles, reveals there is a swift falling off of moral judgment against polygamy. Once again, the great shift in the modern mind-set toward autonomous individualism and moral expressivism has left most of our society without any objective argument against polygamy, so long as all adult parties enter into the relationship with mutual consent. Moreover, the attempt to document social harms by means of sociological analysis runs into the same problems as those encountered by the defenders of traditional marriage. The claim is made that these studies are representative only of the weakest and most extreme forms of such relationships, rather than the consensual strong forms that are now presented, rather attractively, in the nation's media and entertainment culture.

Finally, we need to note that there are some moral revisionists who are openly calling for the acceptance and celebration of polygamy and polyamorous relationships. In 2006, a prominent group of gay liberationists joined in a statement that calls for American society to "move beyond the narrow confines of marriage politics as they exist in the United States today" and give legal recognition and social support for heterosexual couples, same-sex couples, and "committed, loving households in which there is more than one conjugal partner."[6] In other words, this group would include polygamist or polyamorous relationships. Furthermore, they call for the same recognition to "queer couples who decided to jointly create and raise a child with another queer person or couple, in two households," and any number of other arrangements and permutations.[7]

Judith Stacey, professor of social and cultural analysis and sociology at New York University, has also argued in favor of polygamous and polyamorous relationships. Her words represent the sad state of the conversation on marriage in America. In her estimation, the very mission of a democratic society "is to upgrade the menu of love potions on offer and make them available to as many women, and men, as possible."[8] That's what we face in the present moment—"a menu of love potions on offer." It is hard to imagine more heartbreaking words than these—words that point to the end of traditional marriage.

7

WHAT DOES THE BIBLE REALLY HAVE TO SAY ABOUT SEX?

For Christians, the first question to ask when confronting any issue is, what does the Bible say? The answer to this question is fundamental to Christian faith and practice. The ultimate authority for our understanding of reality is the Bible, which is nothing less than the very Word of God. Our knowledge on anything of importance regarding essential questions of life is grounded in the reality that the one true and living God is not only the God who *is* but also the God who *speaks*.

As evangelical theologian Carl F. H. Henry explained so beautifully, God loves us so much that He forfeits His own personal privacy that His creatures might know Him.[1] For this reason, evangelical Christians turn to Scripture by instinct. Going back to the Reformation itself, we live by the principle of *Sola Scriptura*, affirming that Scripture and Scripture alone is our final authority. The reason for this is straightforward. We believe that when Scripture speaks, God speaks. This means that to obey the Scriptures is to obey God and to disobey the Scriptures is to disobey God. Evangelicals can never look at Scripture as just the communication of mere information. The Bible summons us to be obedient and humbly receive what God has revealed to us in his Word.

A Biblical Theology of Sex

This generation has witnessed a renewed understanding of the need to interpret Scripture according to its own internal storyline. This means that we do not look at the Bible as an isolated collection of texts or as a mere communal library for the church, but as a master narrative that from beginning to end situates us in a storyline. Thus, we understand ourselves, the times, the gospel, the church, and the demands of Christian faithfulness and Christian responsibility within the flow of that master narrative—a narrative that passes from creation, to the fall, to redemption, to new creation.

Since Scripture must be interpreted according to this master narrative, when we consider what the Bible says about sex, gender, marriage, and family, we must begin our inquiry in the first act of the biblical story by recognizing that the doctrine of creation provides several essential theological principles for our understanding of sex and gender.

Creation, Gender, and Marriage

The first essential theological principle is the sovereignty of God over all creation. The Creator has the absolute and solitary right to define the purpose of what he has created. As Genesis 1 tells us, human beings, and human beings alone, were created in the image of God. Furthermore, those human beings are gendered—identified as male and female. Together, the man and the woman were given the responsibility to exercise dominion, multiply, and fill the earth. They were given this responsibility as a couple—a husband and wife explicitly charged with procreation as part of their stewardship and ministry.

Genesis 2 provides an even deeper insight into what it means for human beings to be made in the image of God as male and female. Scripture indicates that Adam did not declare his need for a companion; rather, it was God who declared it is not good that man should be alone (Gen. 2:18). Immediately thereafter, God reinforced this point to Adam—in what surely must have been an unforgettable way—by bringing all creatures to Adam so that he might name them. Adam exercised his assignment of dominion by naming the other creatures, but he realized their insufficiency for him. As the Scripture states, "For Adam there was not found a helper fit for him" (v. 20).

At that point, God caused a deep sleep to fall upon Adam and created the woman out of Adam himself (vv. 21–22)—not out of the dust of the earth, and not out of any alien or external substance. Then God presented the woman to Adam as the complementary helper (Hebrew: *ezer*) fit for him. Adam, who had just had the responsibility of naming the animals, then named the woman "Eve," for she had been taken out of man. "This at last is bone of my bones and flesh of my flesh," Adam declared, understanding that Eve was made for him and, correspondingly, he was made for her (v. 23). She was the complement and companion for him. Adam immediately understood the rightness and the fittingness of their exclusive companionship with one another.

Without any transition in the biblical narrative, we are taken to the institution of marriage and told that the pattern from Adam and Eve forward will be that a man will leave his mother and his father, and will *cleave* to his wife (v. 24 KJV). The two then became one flesh. The righteousness of the man and the woman and their unity in a conjugal relationship means that they were naked in the garden and unashamed (v. 25). They were made distinctively male and female with God's glory demonstrated in the maleness of the male and in the femaleness of the female. Further, they were joined together in the conjugal union of marriage and given the divine assignment to multiply and to fill the earth.

The Bible does not present marriage as a "contract," which so many Western societies in the modern age have reduced it to. Rather, Scripture presents marriage as a covenant that reflects God's own covenant-making love in Jesus Christ (Eph. 5:22–33). God's faithfulness in making and keeping his covenants is on display in the lasting covenantal faithfulness of a man and a woman who enter into the monogamous, lifelong union of marriage.

Thus, in the very beginning, human beings are defined as male and female, not just as abstract genders. They are biologically sexed individuals who are created for the glory of God, for each other, and for a conjugal relationship that has as its end the one-flesh relationship of the marital act and the aim of procreation.

Fallen Sexuality

Genesis 3 explains why brokenness exists in the created order. The third chapter of the Bible explains why the universal human experience is one affected by sin, death, and disobedience rather than health and flourishing. Furthermore, the fall helps us understand why every dimension of the created order bears testimony to the effects of human sin and God's judgment upon that sin. In the garden, the one-flesh union of the man and the woman was presented without any stain of sin, any potential embarrassment, or even the slightest insinuation of depravity or corruption. If anything, marriage becomes more important, not less, after the fall. As the traditional Christian wedding language of *The Book of Common Prayer* expresses it, one of the purposes of marriage is to serve as a "remedy for sin." After the fall, marriage and the rightly ordered family become not only a testimony to the goodness of God but also a massive defense against the effects of sin in the world.

Moving forward, the biblical narrative is abundantly honest about the brokenness of humanity. The Bible is straightforward in its depiction of sexual sin—from adultery to incest and bestiality to same-sex behaviors. The Bible's honesty on these matters is an incredible gift to us. Through Scripture, we understand that sin affects every human relationship, even our most intimate relationships—our marriages and families. This portrait of our depravity reveals to us our greatest need—our need of redemption.

Sexuality Redeemed

As Scripture also reveals, God infuses an awareness of his moral law within every one of his image-bearers such that, by common grace, every civilization discovers, to a greater or lesser extent, the need for marriage and respect for the family. At this point, evangelical Christians need to remember that our respect for marriage and the family should not trick us into thinking we can be redeemed by marital faithfulness or family security. Marriage and family joys, even at their height, cannot save us from our sins or protect us from coming judgment. This is why that third act in the biblical metanarrative is vitally important. The doctrine of redemption reminds us that every single human being—whether heterosexual or homosexual—is a sinner in need of the redemption that can only come through Christ.

The redemption Christ provides also reminds us that, as essential as marriage and the family are to human society and human flourishing, there is an even higher allegiance to which believers are called. The church is the family of faith that stands as the bride of Christ and Christ as her bridegroom. This beautiful picture demonstrates the significance of marriage. As the New Testament makes abundantly clear, the moral teachings of the Old Testament law concerning gender, sex, and marriage continue under the new covenant.

Living now under the law of Christ, Christians are called to an even deeper faithfulness. As Jesus taught on the Sermon on the Mount, it is no longer enough that we avoid committing adultery; we are also to abstain from lust. Whereas the Old Testament law focused primarily upon external obedience, the New Testament law demands the obedience of the heart. Scripture reveals that redeemed believers of the Lord Jesus Christ are not capable of obedience to Christ by their own power. Through Christ, we are promised the presence and power of the Holy Spirit in our lives, the conforming power of Holy Scripture, and the fellowship of believers who live together in disciplined faithfulness to the

Lord Jesus Christ, partaking of the means of grace in order that together we may be found faithful.

Thus, out of the reality of a redemption already achieved, Christians are explicitly called to live out what it means to be male and female and lead lives of holiness and righteousness. Marriage is to be honored and is normative for most believers. Those who are unmarried, as the apostle Paul made clear, exercise the gift of celibacy and are able to serve the church in an even greater way by obedience to Christ unhindered by the obligations of marriage and family (1 Cor. 7).

Awaiting Glory: Sexuality and the New Heaven and New Earth

At the same time, we must be very thankful that we are not left as those who are merely washed—we are also waiting. Our sins are forgiven and we now await the new heaven and new earth. According to Scripture, this consummation of history is nothing less than the marriage supper of the Lamb. In the new heaven and new earth, under the lordship of Jesus Christ, all things are made right. Those who are now in Christ will then be with him. In that day, every eye will be dry and every tear will be wiped away.

While gender will remain in the new creation and in our glorified bodies, sexual activity will not. Sex is not nullified in the resurrection, but rather fulfilled. The eschatological marriage supper of the Lamb will finally arrive, to which marriage and sexuality point. There will no longer be any need to fill the earth with image-bearers as there was in Genesis 1. Instead, the earth will be filled with knowledge of the glory of God as the waters cover the sea.

Putting the Pieces Together: Engaging the Sexual Revolution with a Biblical Theology of the Body

In more recent times, evangelicals have learned the necessity of developing an evangelical theology of the body.[2] Given the confusions of our day, we must remember that God has a sovereign purpose for creating us as embodied creatures—creatures that are male and female. Moreover, we must consider that God has given us a bodily structure unique to the man and the woman. An evangelical theology of the body will necessarily challenge one of the fundamental assumptions of the secular age—that our existence as male and female is nothing more than a biological accident brought about by an aimless process of naturalistic evolution. The modern secular mind assumes that our gender is ultimately up to us and that, as the new sexual theorists have been arguing for decades, gender and biology are not necessarily linked. Indeed, the modern assumption is that gender is essentially nothing more than a socially constructed concept that discriminates and oppresses rather than liberates.

The Christian worldview confronts that assumption head-on. Scripture clearly defines human beings as male and female, not by accident, but by divine purpose. Furthermore, this purpose, along with every other aspect of God's creation, is declared by the Creator to be "good." This means that human flourishing and happiness will take place only when the goodness of God's creation is honored as God intended. Having an evangelical theology of the body means that we must affirm the goodness behind male being male and female being female. The brokenness of the world explains why sinners will often either deny the distinctions between the male and the female or exaggerate them beyond what Scripture reveals.

Ideologists of the sexual revolution are partly correct when they argue that much of what our society celebrates as masculine or feminine is the product of social construction. Indeed, as Christians we must remember that Scripture should both inform and correct our notions of masculine and feminine. But, Scripture clearly refutes any theory that promotes gender as only a social construction or that human beings are free to define themselves in a way different than the way God defined them in the act of creation. This means that an evangelical theology of the body begins with the normative understanding that every human being is born biologically assigned as male or female. That biological assignment is not a naturalistic accident, but a sign of God's purpose for that individual human being to display his glory and aim for flourishing and obedience to that creative purpose.

As Scripture also makes clear, the identity of the human being as male and as female points to marriage as the context in which the man and the woman, made for each other, are to come together in a union that is holy, righteous, and absolutely necessary for human flourishing. The scriptural teachings concerning sexuality and marriage show that God made us as sexual beings and gave us sexual feelings, passions, and urges in order that these would be channeled into the desire for marriage and the satisfactions of marital faithfulness.

Sex, gender, marriage, and family all come together in the first chapters of Scripture in order to make clear that every aspect of our sexual lives is to submit to the creative purpose of God and be channeled into the exclusive arena of human sexual behavior—marriage—defined clearly and exclusively as the lifelong, monogamous union of a man and a woman.

The reality of human sinfulness explains why so many of these issues are confused and why we should expect confusion in this world. The effects of sin also explain why there are those deeply troubled about something as fundamental as their gender. A broken world also explains why a very small percentage of human beings are born intersex, that is, born without any clear biological sex.[3] The brokenness of the world also explains why sinners have constructed entire ideologies, theories, and systems of thought in order to justify their sin. This is exactly what Paul indicted in Romans 1 when he described suppressing the truth in unrighteousness and exchanging the truth of God for a lie.

As we read Paul's words in Romans 1, we need to recognize that the apostle Paul was indicting all of humanity in that charge. This means that *all of us*, left to our own devices, suppress the truth in unrighteousness and justify our own sin by creating our own rationalizations. We are rescued from that process of fatal self-deception only by the revelation of God in Holy Scripture and by the victory of Christ in his cross and resurrection. It is urgently important that Christians affirm we are not smarter or more morally righteous than those around us. We are instead the beneficiaries of the grace and mercy of God because we have come to know salvation through Christ, and guidance in faithful living through the gift of Holy Scripture.

Christians guided by Scripture recognize current controversies and confusions over sex, marriage, and other issues of importance as part of what it means to live in a fallen world. This also reveals why the church in its distinctive witness must honor the good gifts God gives us, just as Scripture instructs us, in order to accomplish two great purposes. The first of these purposes is to obey God and to find true happiness and human flourishing as we obey. The second purpose is that we live out that obedience before a watching world so that others may see the glory of God in the Christian's faithfulness in marriage and every other dimension of life so that others who need Christ may find him.

The Christian's faithfulness in marriage and faithful defense of marriage and gender is an act of Christian witness—indeed, one of the boldest acts of Christian witness in this secular age. The final chapter of Scripture reminds us that we will struggle with human brokenness and the effects of human sin until Jesus comes. Until then, we are to be found both washed and waiting, eager for the redemption of our bodies and for the fullness of the kingdom of the Lord Jesus Christ.

The Christian understanding of the Bible's metanarrative and a biblical theology of the body, sex, and marriage is foundational to dealing with the questions now forced upon us by the theological revisionists demanding that we reconsider—or reject—Scripture's clear condemnation of homosexuality. Now—and only now—are we able to turn to those specific questions and do so in the context of a truly biblical theology.

Twisting the Truth: Homosexuality and the Revisionist Theologians

As the legitimization of homosexuality gains public prominence, some churches and denominations have joined the movement—even becoming advocates of homosexuality—while others steadfastly refuse to compromise. In the middle—for now—are churches and denominations unable or unwilling to declare a clear conviction on homosexuality. Issues of homosexual ordination and marriage are discussed regularly in the assemblies of several denominations—and many congregations.

The challenge for the believing church now comes down to this: Do we have a distinctive message in the midst of this moral confusion?

Our answer must be *yes*. The Christian church must have a distinctive message to say to the issue of homosexuality because faithfulness to Holy Scripture demands it.

The affirmation of biblical authority is central to the church's consideration of this issue or any other issue. The Bible is the Word of God in written form, inerrant and infallible, inspired by the Holy Spirit "for teaching, for reproof, for correction, and for training in righteousness" (2 Tim. 3:16). This is the critical watershed: those churches that reject the authority of Scripture will eventually succumb to cultural pressure and accommodate their understanding of homosexuality to the spirit of the age. Those churches that affirm, confess, and acknowledge the full authority of the Bible have no choice in this matter—we must speak a word of compassionate truth. And that compassionate truth is this: homosexual acts are expressly and unconditionally forbidden by God through his Word, and such acts are an abomination to the Lord by his own declaration.

As this entire book has demonstrated, the momentum to normalize homosexuality is driven by an ideology totally committed to the cause of making homosexuality a sanctioned and recognized form of sexual activity. Every obstacle that stands in the way of progress toward this agenda must be removed. God's Word stands as the most formidable obstacle to that agenda.

We should not be surprised that apologists for the homosexual agenda have entered the world of biblical scholarship. Biblical scholars are themselves a mixed group. Some defend the authority of Scripture while others are bent on deconstructing it. The battle lines on this issue are immediately apparent. Many who deny the truthfulness, inspiration, and authority of the Bible argue that Scripture sanctions homosexuality—or at least argue that the biblical passages forbidding homosexual acts are confused, misinterpreted, or irrelevant.

To accomplish this requires feats of acrobatic biblical interpretation worthy of the most agile circus contortionist. Several decades ago, the late J. Gresham Machen remarked, "The Bible, with a complete abandonment of all scientific historical method, and of all common sense, is made to say the exact opposite of what it means; no Gnostic, no medieval monk with his fourfold sense of Scripture, ever produced more absurd Biblical interpretation than can be heard every Sunday in the pulpits of New York."[4] Machen was referring to the misuse and misapplication of Scripture that he saw as a mark of the infusion of a pagan spirit within the church. Even greater absurdity than what Machen observed is now evident among those determined to interpret the Bible as sanctioning homosexuality.

Biblical Christianity is the final wall of resistance to the homosexual agenda. In the end, that resistance comes down to the Bible itself. Those working tirelessly for the normalization of homosexuality know that the Bible's clear and unambiguous opposition to all forms of homosexual behavior must be neutralized if they are to be fully successful. Their efforts to this end deserve our closest attention.

The theological revisionists have employed several different interpretive strategies in their effort to overcome the Bible's clear testimony to the sinfulness of same-sex behaviors. For some theological revisionists, an outright rejection of biblical authority is explicit. Consider, for example, Dan O. Via's comments in *Homosexuality and the Bible: Two Views*. Via, opposing the arguments of Robert Gagnon, who defends the traditional understanding of homosexuality in that same book, stated, "[Gagnon's] accumulation of biblical texts condemning homosexual practice is irrelevant to my argument since I agree that Scripture gives no explicit approval to same-sex intercourse. I maintain, however, that the absolute prohibition can be overridden regardless of how many times it is stated, for there are good reasons to override it."[5]

Similarly, with astounding candor, William M. Kent, a member of the committee assigned by United Methodists to study homosexuality, declared, "The scriptural texts in the Old and New Testaments condemning homosexual practice are neither inspired by God nor otherwise of enduring Christian value. Considered in the light of the best biblical, theological, scientific, and social knowledge, the biblical condemnation of homosexual practice is better understood as representing time and place bound cultural prejudice."[6]

This approach is the most honest taken among the revisionists. Those who push this approach do not deny that the Bible expressly forbids homosexual practices—they acknowledge the Bible does just that. Their answer is straightforward: the Bible must be abandoned in light of modern knowledge.

In a nutshell, that is where the argument really stands. It is not an argument over what the biblical text says, but over the authority of the biblical text and the proper means of obeying it. Evangelicals should immediately recognize that the premise of obeying Scripture by transcending its clear meaning is not only suspect but also fallacious. This is the critical distinction between what may be called a hermeneutic of suspicion, and a hermeneutic of submission and obedience. The hermeneutic of suspicion, rooted in the Enlightenment and modern skepticism, approaches the Bible with the assumption that it must be interpreted in light of present needs, which means it may mean something today that it did not mean in the past. A hermeneutic of submission, on the other hand, looks at the Bible as the written Word of God and seeks to understand the Scripture in order to faithfully obey it. A hermeneutic of submission forbids the reader to use an interpretive device in order to escape the trap of the text—which is exactly what the revisionist biblical scholars and their disciples are trying to do.

Another approach taken by the revisionists is to suggest that the human authors of Scripture were limited by the scientific immaturity of their age. One example of this type of theological revisionism is found in Matthew Vines's *God and the Gay Christian*.[7] One of Vines's main arguments is that the Bible simply has no category of sexual orientation. Thus, when the Bible condemns same-sex acts, it is actually condemning "sexual excess," hierarchy, oppression, or abuse—not the possibility of permanent, monogamous, same-sex unions.

In fact, throughout his book, Vines returns to sexual orientation as the key issue. "The Bible doesn't directly address the issue of same-sex *orientation*," he insists.[8] The concept of sexual orientation "didn't exist in the ancient world."[9] Amazingly, he then concedes that the Bible's "six references to same-sex behavior are negative," but insists again that "the concept of same-sex behavior in the Bible is sexual excess, not sexual orientation."[10]

But if the modern concept of sexual orientation is taken as a brute fact, then the Bible simply cannot be trusted to understand what it means to be human, to reveal what God intends for us sexually, or to define sin in any coherent manner. The modern notion of sexual orientation is actually exceedingly modern. It is also a concept without any definitive meaning. Effectively, it is used now both culturally and morally to argue about sexual attraction and desire. As a matter of fact, attraction and desire are the only indicators upon which modern notions of sexual orientation are premised.

At the beginning of his book, Vines argues that experience should not drive our interpretation of the Bible. But it is his experience of what he calls a gay sexual orientation that drives every word of his argument. It is this experiential issue that drives him to relativize text after text and to argue that the Bible really does not speak directly to his sexual identity at all, since the inspired human authors of Scripture were ignorant of the modern gay experience.

Vines claims to hold to a "high view" of the Bible and to believe that "all of Scripture is inspired by God and authoritative for my life,"[11] but the modern concept of sexual orientation functions as a much higher authority in his thinking and in his argument.

This leads to a haunting question. What else does the Bible not know about being human? If the Bible cannot be trusted to reveal the truth about us in every respect, how can we trust it to reveal our salvation?

This points to the greater issue at stake here—the gospel. Revisionist arguments that focus on the "limitations" of Scripture do not merely relativize the Bible's authority—they leave us without any authoritative revelation of what sin is. And without an authoritative (and clearly understandable) revelation of human sin, we cannot know why we need a Savior or why Christ died. Could the stakes be any higher than that? This controversy is not merely about sex. It is about salvation.

Trusting the Truth: The Path of True Discipleship

With the movement toward same-sex marriage and the normalization of homosexuality gaining momentum, some churches are running for cover. Yet our Christian responsibility is clear—we are to tell the truth about what God has revealed concerning human sexuality, gender, and marriage. No one said it was going to be easy.

At every point the confessing and believing church runs counter to the cultural tidal wave. Even raising the issue of gender is an offense to those who wish to eradicate gender distinctions, arguing they are merely "socially constructed realities" and vestiges of an ancient past.

Scripture forbids this attempt to remove the infrastructure of creation. We must read Romans 1 in light of Genesis 1–2. As Genesis 1:27 makes clear, God intended from the beginning to create human beings as two genders or sexes—"male and female he created them." Man and woman are both created in the image of God. They are distinct, and yet inseparably linked by God's design. The genders are different. Their distinctions go far beyond mere physical differences, but the man recognized "bone of my bones and flesh of my flesh" (Gen. 2:23) in the woman.

The bond between man and woman is marriage, which is not a historical accident or the result of gradual socialization. To the contrary, marriage and the establishment of the heterosexual covenant union is central to God's intention—before and after the fall. Immediately following the creation of man and woman come the instructive words: "Therefore a man shall leave his father and his mother and hold fast to his wife, and they shall become one flesh. And the man and his wife were both naked and were not ashamed" (vv. 24–25).

Evangelicals have often failed to present this biblical truth straightforwardly. As a result, many of our churches are unprepared for the ideological, political, and cultural conflicts that mark the modern landscape. The fundamental axiom upon which evangelical Christians must base every response to homosexuality is this: God alone is sovereign, and he alone created the universe and everything within it by his own design and for his own good pleasure. Furthermore, he showed us his creative intention through Holy Scripture—and that intention is clearly to create and establish two distinct but complementary genders or sexes. The Genesis narrative demonstrates that this distinction of genders is neither accidental nor inconsequential to the divine design.

God's creative intention is further revealed in the cleaving of man to the woman ("his wife") and their new identity as "one flesh" (Gen. 2:24). This biblical assertion, which no contorted interpretation can escape, clearly places marriage and sexual relations within God's creative act and design.

The sexual union of a man and a woman in covenant marriage is thus not only allowed, but also commanded as God's intention and decree. Sexual expression is limited to this heterosexual covenant, which in its clearest biblical expression is one man and one woman united for as long as they both shall live.

Therefore, any sexual expression outside of that heterosexual marriage relationship is outlawed by God's command. That fundamental truth runs counter not only to the homosexual agenda but to the rampant sexual immorality of the age. Indeed, the Bible has much more to say about illicit heterosexual activity than it does about homosexual acts.

As E. Michael Jones argued, most modern ideologies are basically efforts to rationalize sexual behavior. In fact, he identifies modernity itself as "rationalized lust."[12] We should expect the secular world, which is at war with God's truth, to be eager in its efforts to rationalize lust, and to seek legitimacy and social sanction for its sexual sins. On the other hand, we should be shocked to see many within the church seeking to accomplish the same purpose and allying with those openly at war with God's truth.

Paul's classic statement in Romans 1 sets the issues squarely before us. Homosexuality is linked directly to idolatry, for it is because of their idolatry that God gave them up to their own lusts. Their hearts were committed to impurity, and they were degrading their own bodies by their illicit lusts.

Their idolatry—exchanging the truth of God for a lie, and worshipping the creature rather than the Creator—led God to give them over to their degrading passions. From here, those given over to their degraded passions exchanged the natural use of sexual intercourse for what God declared unnatural. At this point, Paul was dealing explicitly with female homosexuality. This is one of the very few references to female homosexuality in all of ancient literature, but Paul's message is clear.

The women involved in lesbianism were not and are not alone. Men, too, had forfeited natural intercourse with women and have been consumed with passion for other men. The acts they commit are without shame. As a result, they received the penalty for their idolatry within their own bodies.

The biblical witness is clear. Homosexuality is a sin against God and a direct rejection of God's intention and command in creation. All sin is a matter of eternal consequence. The redemption accomplished by Jesus Christ is the only hope for sinners. On the cross, Jesus paid the price for our sins and served as the substitute for the redeemed.

Our response to persons involved in homosexuality must be marked by genuine compassion. But a central task of genuine compassion is telling the truth, and the Bible reveals a true message we must convey. Those contorting and subverting the Bible's message are not responding to homosexuals with compassion. Lying is never compassionate—and ultimately leads to death.

In the end, the church will either declare the truth of God's Word, or it will find a way to run away from it. It ultimately comes down to *trust*. Do we trust the Bible to tell us truthfully what God desires and commands about our sexuality? If so, we know where we stand and we know what to say. If not, it is time we admit to the world that we do not have the slightest clue.

8

RELIGIOUS LIBERTY AND THE
RIGHT TO BE CHRISTIAN

Moral revolutions require legal revolutions. This is certainly the case with the sexual revolution and its various causes of sexual liberation. A revolution is only complete when the legal structure aligns itself with a new moral understanding. This alignment is exactly what is taking place in American public life on the issue of gay liberation.

Every society has a structure of systems that either influences or coerces behavior. Eventually, societies move to legislate and regulate behavior in order to align the society with what is commonly, or at least largely, considered morally right and wrong. Civilization could not survive without a system of moral controls and influences.

Throughout almost all Western history, for the most part, this process has played out in a nonthreatening way for the Christian church and Christians in the larger society. So long as the moral judgment of the culture matched the convictions and teachings of the church, the church and culture were not at odds in the courts. Furthermore, under these conditions, to be found on the wrong side of a moral assessment was rarely a likelihood for Christians.

All that began to change in the modern age as the culture became more secularized and as Western societies moved more progressively distant from the Christian morality they had embraced in the past. Christians in this generation recognize that we do not represent the same moral framework now pervasively presented in modern academia, the context of creative culture, and the arena of law. The secularization of public life and the separation of society from its Christian roots have left many Americans seemingly unaware of the fact that the very beliefs and teachings for which Christians are now criticized were once considered not only mainstream beliefs, but essential to the entire project of society. As the sexual revolution completely pervades the society, and as the issues raised by the efforts of gay liberation and the legalization of same-sex marriage come to the fore, Christians now face an array of religious liberty challenges that were inconceivable in previous generations.

Before turning to the specific issues raised by the sexual revolution and same-sex marriage, we need to think about the controversy that transpired in America over the contraception mandate in the Affordable Care Act that led to the U.S. Supreme Court's Hobby Lobby decision in the summer of 2014. In that 5–4 decision, the Court ruled that Hobby Lobby and Conestoga Wood Specialties, privately held companies founded and managed by Christian families, had a religious liberty right to refuse to include coverage for drugs that might function as abortifacients in their health care plans for employees. More than the case itself, the reaction to the court's decision is both illuminating and deeply concerning. The secular culture has responded with outright alarm and indignation that the court would rule that these two companies have the right to defy the prevailing wisdom of the contraception movement and the government's efforts to coerce their participation. Furthermore, the court's decision was by a 5–4 vote among the nine justices, indicating that the shift of just one justice's judgment would have led to the opposite conclusion—that fact should focus our concern.

The Hobby Lobby case did not emerge in a vacuum, and the cause of the controversy was not directly related to homosexuality or same-sex marriage. Nevertheless, the contours of the argument presented by both sides in this case and the response of the secular elites to the court's decision reveal what Christians already face in light of the challenges posed by the normalization of homosexuality and the legalization of same-sex marriage.

Just consider the following controversies that have erupted recently in the news. Government authorities have declared florists, wedding photographers, and cake bakers guilty of violating nondiscrimination laws. In some of these cases, courts or administrative agencies have declared them guilty. Their offense is exercising and protecting their Christian conscience by refusing to participate in the celebration of what they consider sin—a same-sex wedding. In almost all these cases, the courts have found that the religious liberty of the individual must give way to the larger societal purpose of reinforcing the new morality.[1]

In one of the most important of these recent cases, a judge found that a wedding photographer broke the law by refusing to serve as a photographer for a same-sex wedding. In an incredibly revealing decision, the court stated, quite straightforwardly, that the religious liberties of the photographer would indeed be violated by coerced participation in a same-sex wedding. Nevertheless, the court found that the new morality trumped concern for religious liberty.[2]

Similarly, we have seen religious institutions, especially colleges and schools, confronted by the demands that amount to a surrender to the sexual revolution with regards to nondiscrimination on the basis of sex, sexual behavior, and sexual orientation pertaining to admissions, the hiring of faculty, and student housing. In some jurisdictions, lawmakers are contemplating hate-crime legislation that would marginalize and criminalize speech that is in conflict with the new moral consensus.

In other cases, Christian couples are finding that adoption and foster care are increasingly difficult because the new moral authorities require "nonjudgmentalism" concerning sexual orientation and identity. Churches and Christian organizations are increasingly pushed to the margins of American social life and disadvantaged in their public influence and participation in public activities. Gordon College, an evangelical Christian college in Massachusetts, which had leased space from the city government, was informed that the privilege would be terminated, simply because the college's president signed a private letter calling for President Obama to recognize the rights of religious institutions in antidiscrimination regulations.

Related to that controversy, the Obama administration handed down regulations requiring all entities contracting with the federal government to adhere, without exception, to absolute nondiscrimination on the basis of sexual orientation and gender identity. A plethora of state and local governments are acting in similar ways. They are banning the participation of any organization that refuses to be publicly committed to absolute nondiscrimination concerning sexual orientation, gender, and gender identity.

The arrival of same-sex marriage as a legal reality presents immediate challenges to religious liberty. In the state of Massachusetts, a venerable and respected charitable organization was forced to stop its work of placing children and infants through adoption because it refused to violate church teachings by accepting a total nondiscrimination policy on sexual orientation. These cases are only the leading edge of a massive reorientation of American public life and American law.

We also need to recognize that the law is not the only instrument of legal coercion. Coercion can come in regulations undertaken by voluntary associations. Religious colleges and universities participating in intercollegiate athletics are likely soon to discover that groups such as the NCAA will come under pressure to exclude any institution that discriminates on sexual orientation from participation. Accrediting agencies, some of which have long been in an internal struggle to accommodate Christian institutions within their existing nondiscrimination policies, will come under increased pressure to eliminate from membership any school that discriminates in any way on the basis of sexual orientation or gender identity in the admission of students, the discipline of students, student housing, and the hiring of faculty.

Religious Liberty and the Challenge of Same-Sex Marriage

This revolution in the law comes as no surprise. Even though same-sex marriage is new to the American scene, the religious liberty challenges became fully apparent even before it became a reality. Soon after the legalization of same-sex marriage in the state of Massachusetts, several seminars and symposia were held in order to consider the religious liberty dimensions of this legal revolution. In 2005, the Becket Fund for Religious Liberty sponsored one of the most important of these events, and the consensus of every single participant in the conference was that the normalization of homosexuality and the legalization of same-sex marriage would produce a head-on collision in the courts. As Marc D. Stern of the American Jewish Congress stated, "Same-sex marriage would work a sea change in American law. That change will reverberate across the legal and religious landscape in ways that are unpredictable today."[3]

Even then, Stern saw almost all the issues we have recounted and others yet to come. He saw the campuses of religious colleges and the work of religious institutions as inevitable arenas of legal conflict. He pointed to employment as one of the crucial issues of legal conflict and spoke with pessimism about the ability of religious institutions to maintain liberty in this context. As Stern argued, "The legalization of same-sex marriage would represent the triumph of an egalitarian-based ethic over a faith-based one, and not just legally. The remaining question is whether champions of tolerance are prepared to tolerate proponents of a different ethical vision. I think the answer will be no."[4]

Other legal scholars verified Stern's assessment as well. Chai R. Feldblum—a lesbian activist who has advocated for same-sex marriage and for the legalization of polygamy—offered rare candor in describing "the conflict that . . . exists between laws intended to protect the liberty of lesbian, gay, bisexual, and transgender (LGBT) people so that they may live lives of dignity and integrity and the religious beliefs of some individuals whose conduct is regulated by such laws."[5] She went on to state her belief that "those who advocate for LGBT equality have downplayed the impact of such laws on some people's religious beliefs and, equally, I believe those who sought religious exemptions from such civil rights laws have downplayed the impact that such exemptions would have on LGBT people."[6]

Appointed and later confirmed as a commissioner of the U.S. Equal Employment Opportunity Commission, Feldblum stated in a different context that the end result of antidiscrimination legislation would mean the victory of sexual rights over religious liberty. She commented that she could not come up with a *single case* in which, even hypothetically, religious liberty should triumph over coercion to the new moral morality.

In other words, there must be no exceptions. Religious liberty simply evaporates as a fundamental right grounded in the U.S. Constitution, and recedes into the background in the wake of what is now a higher social commitment—sexual freedom.

Conflict of Liberties: Religious Liberty v. Erotic Liberty

We now face an inevitable conflict of liberties. In this context of acute and radical moral change, the conflict of liberties is excruciating, immense, and eminent. In this case, the conflict of liberties means that the new moral regime, with the backing of the courts and the regulatory state, will prioritize erotic liberty over religious liberty. Over the course of the last several decades, we have seen this revolution coming. Erotic liberty has been elevated as a right more fundamental than religious liberty. Erotic liberty now marginalizes, subverts, and neutralizes religious liberty—a liberty highly prized by the builders of this nation and its constitutional order. We must remember that the framers of the Constitution did not believe they were creating rights within the Constitution; rather, they were acknowledging rights given to all humanity by "nature and nature's God."

Erotic liberty emerges directly from arguments made in opinions handed down by the United States Supreme Court. The *Griswold* decision and William O. Douglas's "finding" of the right to privacy, and thus a right to birth-control pills within the Fourteenth Amendment of the United States Constitution, laid much of the groundwork for the advancement of erotic liberty. As Douglas acknowledged, this right is by no means explicit or even present in the text of the Constitution. It is extracted from the words of the Constitution. Similarly, in the *Planned Parenthood of Southeastern Pennsylvania v. Casey* decision on abortion in 1992, Justices Sandra Day O'Connor, Anthony Kennedy, and David Souter declared, "At the heart of liberty is the right to define one's own concept of existence, of meaning, of the universe, and of the mystery of human life"[7]—a definition of liberty that also influenced the 2003 *Lawrence v. Texas* decision that struck down all laws against sodomy.

The use of that language demonstrates how erotic liberty typifies the freedom most cherished by the culture and most respected by the courts in the context of the secular age. A liberty that did not even exist when the Constitution was written, even in the imagination of the founders, now supersedes protections that are explicit in the Constitution. This explains the trajectory of court decisions and developments in the law and, at the same time, reveals the trajectory we can expect to be extended even further in the future.

Religious Liberty and Accusations of "Hate Speech"

Taken at face value, the direction of the courts raises the specter of laws against speech. The notion of "hate speech" has emerged in recent years as a way of proposing either moral regulations or laws that would prohibit certain speech in the public square because it might be considered derogatory to an individual or a minority. In both Europe and Canada, hate speech laws have been used to sanction and criminalize Christian speech, regardless if a pastor in the pulpit or an individual Christian in the public square is doing the talking.

American Christians often assume that the First Amendment to the United States Constitution and its guarantee of free speech will be ample legal defense against similar developments in the United States. A response to this must begin by acknowledging that the United States Constitution's First Amendment guarantee of free speech is itself a powerfully straightforward statement with massive societal support. But lest Christians take too much comfort in that security, we must remember that this same First Amendment that guarantees free speech also guarantees religious liberty— and we are now fairly aware that religious liberty is anything but secure.

We should also recognize that the logic of hate speech legislation does not extend only to actions undertaken by government. The logic of hate speech legislation is being increasingly adopted on college and university campuses. Whereas in previous generations speech was pervasively regulated by what was called "political correctness," that same logic is now being extended, most decisively, against any speech that would imply a negative moral judgment on the LGBT community or other sexual minorities. Similarly, classroom codes of speech in many American public schools impose the same guidelines on students.

In this country, cases have arrived at the courts concerning the right of Christian children and teenagers to wear a T-shirt that may have nothing more than a Bible verse or a statement affirming heterosexuality on it. The same logic leading educators in nations such as Sweden and Canada to ban the use of gendered personal pronouns is leading many teachers and educators in American school districts to censure and monitor speech in order to avoid any language (even the use of the words *girlfriend* and *boyfriend*) that could be considered harmful in any way to an individual in the classroom. On American college and university campuses, some teachers and students are even demanding professors issue "trigger warnings" when bringing up certain subjects of sensitivity as to give advance notice to students who might be traumatized, even by academic lectures related to sex or sexual orientation (among other things) in the context of the classroom.

Even while religious liberty is supposedly recognized and affirmed, it is often being transformed and minimized. The Obama administration provides a classic example of this. Numerous representatives of the administration, including President Obama himself, have shifted their language from "freedom of religion" to "freedom of worship." Though these two phrases may appear to be very similar, freedom of worship is a severe and deadly reduction of freedom of religion. Religious freedom is not limited to what takes place within the confines of a church building and its worship. Freedom of worship marginalizes and ghettoizes Christian speech so that its liberties only exist within the confines of a church facility—but it does not guarantee a right to a public voice. Freedom of worship essentially muzzles the Christian in the public square.[8]

Recent Challenges to Religious Liberty

Several early challenges to religious liberty came in the months following the Supreme Court's *Windsor* decision. In October 2014, Mayor Annise Parker of Houston led an effort to adopt an antidiscrimination law that, among other things, allowed transgender persons to file a complaint and bring charges if they were denied access to a bathroom.

Several Houston-area pastors were involved in an effort to rescind the ordinance. They participated in a petition drive that would have put the question before voters, mobilizing their congregations on the issue. They were able to get more than the required number of signatures on the petition, but the city attorney ruled many of the signatures invalid due to technicalities. The city attorney intervened after the appropriate city official had already certified the petitions as adequate. This set the stage for the lawsuit, and the lawsuit set the stage for the subpoenas.

The very fact that the subpoenas were issued at all was scandal enough—none of the pastors were even party to the lawsuit. But the actual wording of the subpoenas was draconian—almost unbelievable. The attorneys working for the city demanded all sermons "prepared by, delivered by, revised by, or approved by you or in your possession" on matters that included not only the mayor and the ordinance but homosexuality and gender identity.[9]

This was a breathtaking violation of religious liberty—and an instance of political thuggery at its worst. A major American city attempted to subpoena the sermons of Christian pastors. And those sermons were to include anything that even touched on homosexuality or gender identity.

The fact that the subpoenas were eventually withdrawn under public pressure does nothing to remove the fact that they were issued and stood for a matter of weeks. By any measure, the Houston incident serves as a dramatic alert to the fact that infringements and violations of religious liberty are very close at hand.

Just weeks later, Kelvin Cochran, chief of Atlanta's Fire Rescue Department, was fired after writing a book in which he affirmed that the Bible condemned homosexual acts. Atlanta's mayor, Kasim Reed, took such extreme actions against Chief Cochran even though there was no accusation that he had acted in a discriminatory fashion toward any department employee. Mayor Reed indicated that Chief Cochran's views as expressed in the book were inconsistent with the city's policies on discrimination. Mayor Reed stated, "I want to be clear that the material in Chief Cochran's book is not representative of my personal beliefs, and is inconsistent with the administration's work to make Atlanta a more welcoming city for all of her citizens—regardless of their sexual orientation, gender, race and religious beliefs."[10] The mayor did not, however, extend his concern about nondiscrimination on religious beliefs to Chief Cochran, who clearly expressed his views as a matter of biblical belief.

The debacle of the subpoenaed sermons in Houston and the firing of Chief Cochran is a picture of things to come. This is how religious liberty dies—by a thousand cuts. An intimidating letter here, a subpoena there, a warning in yet another place. The message is simple and easily understood. Be quiet and get in line or risk trouble.

Religious Liberty in the Balance

The challenges we will face with regard to religious liberty are immense and increasing by the season. The government has at its disposal mechanisms for moral coercion that reach far beyond prisons, jails, and fines. For example, a few businesspeople who refused to participate in same-sex weddings, such as photographers, bakers, or florists, were required to undergo "sensitivity training." To understand how the new moral regime uses sensitivity training, it is helpful to think back to iconic works of the twentieth century, such as Aldous Huxley's *Brave New World* and George Orwell's *1984*. These sensitivity-training programs represent efforts to bring intellectual cleansing. And now, in some jurisdictions they can be inflicted upon religious believers who dare oppose the morality of the new regime.

Nevertheless, the same mechanisms of thought control and conformity are affecting far more Americans as they enter our nation's colleges and universities. On today's average state university campus, as well as in elite private institutions, freshmen are required to sit through hours of sensitivity training and moral indoctrination on the new morality of campus sex codes. In almost every case, this indoctrination involves instruction on the only acceptable way of thinking and speaking about the LGBT community and other sexual minorities.

The trajectory of the federal courts is now clear. By the time the U.S. Supreme Court handed down its rulings in the Proposition 8 case and the legal challenge to the Defense of Marriage Act, the momentum toward the total normalization of homosexuality and the legalization of same-sex marriage was at breakneck speed. When the *Windsor* decision was handed down in 2013, Justice Antonin Scalia announced that the imposition of legalized same-sex marriage coast to coast was now inevitable. He accused Justice Anthony Kennedy, who wrote the decision's majority opinion, and his colleagues of failing in their willingness to state this boldly. As Justice Scalia anticipated, all we are waiting for now is for the shoe to drop.[11]

Justice Scalia asserted that the succession of cases representing the progress of the gay liberation movement effectively meant the end of all morals legislation. But he was wrong on one account. The present trajectory of the courts means the end of all morals legislation that American society recognized just a matter of decades ago. We can anticipate *new* morals legislation put into place that will reinforce the significant gains made by the sexual liberationists. Christians and other religious citizens will have to pay careful attention as these new laws are established, for religious liberty will be at stake and at risk in each of them.

The "take no prisoners" approach now demanded by the moral liberationists and increasingly accepted by the courts means that any exceptions are likely to be tenuous and narrow, even when laws and regulations supposedly allow "religious exceptions." We have already seen this in the contraception mandate in the Affordable Care Act. Authorities within the Obama administration and the Department of Health and Human Services spoke of religious exemption only in terms of "houses of worship," again demonstrating the determination to narrow freedom of religion to freedom of worship.

The religious liberty challenge we now face consigns every believer, every religious institution, and every congregation in the arena of conflict where erotic liberty and religious liberty now clash. This poses no danger to theological liberals and their churches and denominations because those churches have accommodated themselves to the new morality and find themselves quite comfortable within the context of the new moral regime. Furthermore, some of these liberal denominations and churches style themselves as defenders of the new morality and actually advocate legal modifications that restrict the religious liberty rights of more conservative churches and denominations.

The arenas of conflict are already numerous and multiplying. Christian colleges and universities will face the immediate threat of being further marginalized in the larger culture. Some will be threatened with the denial of accreditation and labeled outlaws simply because they remain true to historic Christian conviction and biblical accountability. Given the fact that accrediting agencies and organizations such as the NCAA are identified as voluntary associations, they can make a legal claim to discriminate on that basis. But the "voluntary" nature of organizations such as regional accrediting agencies is undermined by the fact that, in many jurisdictions, colleges and universities are required to have such accreditation in order to have legal authority to conduct their programs.

Christian churches must also be aware of the threat represented by the sexual revolution. The church's freedom is not only the freedom to preach and teach within the confines of its worship service. Even as there are those now arguing to restrict or sanction speech by preachers, the more pressing threat is that the ministry of the church will be constricted by means of other regulations and discriminatory policies. Christians in the business world must watch carefully as legislation such as the Employment Nondiscrimination Act (ENDA) comes into view.

Without protection for religious liberty and Christian conscience, these laws will be used in a way that requires many Christians in business to decide between compromising conviction or going out of business.

Employees and executives in many corporations and American institutions already face this threat. They must either endorse the new moral regime or get out of the way. Christian humanitarian organizations face being cut off from access to ministry, unless they endorse the new sexual morality and operate by its precepts. Students in public schools face the denial of religious liberty rights and free association rights. Christian couples may well face severe headwinds as they attempt to adopt children. These are not idle threats or issues of hypothetical concern. Every one of these threats is rooted in arguments already made in the public square or political and legal processes already in play.

Interestingly, Jonathan Rauch, one of the early advocates of gay marriage, warned his fellow moral revolutionaries that they must be careful lest they trample upon the conscience rights and religious liberty of their adversaries. In his book *Kindly Inquisitors: The New Attacks on Free Thought*, Rauch voiced his concern: "Today I fear that many people on my side of the gay-equality question are forgetting our debt to the system that freed us. Some gay people—not all, not even most, but quite a few—want to expunge discriminatory views. 'Discrimination is discrimination and bigotry is bigotry,' they say, 'and they are intolerable whether or not they happen to be someone's religion or moral creed.'"[12]

Rauch also stated, "I hope that when gay people—and non-gay people—encounter hateful or discriminatory opinions, we respond not by trying to silence or punish them but by trying to correct them."[13] Very few signs, however, are signaling that Rauch's admonition is being heard. A review of the religious liberty challenges already confronting the conscience, conduct, and belief rights of convictional Christians shows us how daunting all this really is. We can be sure this is not the end of our struggle. It is only the beginning.

9

THE COMPASSION OF TRUTH: THE CHURCH AND THE CHALLENGE OF THE SEXUAL REVOLUTION

The sexual revolution presents a monumental challenge to the Christian church, but this is not the first revolution that has demanded a Christian response. In this new age, however, the church faces a revolution different from those of the past. As we have seen, this moral revolution challenges the very heart of Christian conviction. We have also seen that this revolution did not erupt out of a vacuum. Decades of intellectual shift and social change preceded this revolution and made it possible, if not inevitable. Furthermore, we must recognize that as the sexual revolution gains more and more traction in the court of public opinion, the church will continue to be displaced in the larger culture.

Sociologists identify the trajectory of our culture in terms of secularization and its effects. As cultures develop and become more industrialized and technologically advanced, theism retreats and the public space becomes increasingly devoid of theological conviction. The modern age has brought us both peril and promise, offering technological goods and social advances that Christians celebrate and utilize. At the same time, the modern age has opened the door to a new morality that biblical Christians believe will threaten, rather than enhance, human dignity and human flourishing.

For Christians in the United States (and evangelical Christians in particular) this revolution turns the world upside down. Evangelicals in this country are accustomed to social respect and credibility. We have had access to cultural arenas of influence, even if we understood that we were often only guests within those contexts. Yet we were welcome, and we trusted that our voice and message were respected.

All that has now changed. In one sense, we might count much of what has been lost as peripheral and ceremonial. The last several decades make it hard to imagine a presidential inauguration in which an evangelical figure does not play at least a ceremonial part. As we saw with Pastor Louie Giglio in 2013, however, any Christian pastor who has preached a message declaring homosexuality to be sinful is now disqualified in many eyes.[1] There was a day when it was politically inconceivable to imagine an evangelical figure such as Billy Graham not getting invited to the White House or to participate in the inauguration of the president of the United States. That day has passed. Now a pastor faithful to the Bible's teaching on sexuality and marriage is not likely to stand on the inaugural platform. That is how fast the world has changed.

In the eyes of the secular world, Christians—and evangelicals in particular—are increasingly an embarrassment. Even more hauntingly, some of us have become embarrassments to our own children. Many in the millennial generation are committed to what some scholars call the "eleventh commandment" of our culture: *Thou shalt not be intolerant.* Christian convictions on human sexuality are now seen and dismissed as out-of-date, out of step, and out of line. In response, many evangelical parents, pastors, and leaders are seemingly retreating into silence, if not total surrender. As one pastor told me a few years ago, "I have a position on homosexuality, but my church doesn't know what it is."

The church must recognize that the sexual revolution has vastly transformed our society, especially in the last several decades. We should expect horrifying harm, the decline of human flourishing, and restrictions on our message and the freedom of the Christian church. At the same time, we must recognize that a gospel people—that is, a truly evangelical church—will look at this challenge as an opportunity, even as it recognizes it as a tragic reality.

If nothing else, the new morality of a post-Christian culture frees us from our delusional confidence that the people around us, though Christless, are somehow Christians—or will at least act like Christians. Evangelicals have mistakenly drawn continual confidence from polls indicating that the vast majority of Americans were Christians in general, and evangelicals in particular. We have considered ourselves as dominant within the culture, especially within the Bible Belt and other areas of concentrated evangelical influence. Yet we have fooled ourselves into believing that our neighbors are fellow believers, even when they have no cognitive commitment to the Christian faith and no active sign of Christian discipleship.

Now we see cultural Christianity disappearing as fast as a morning mist. The cultural authorities are dismissing biblical Christianity with condescension or worse. As identifying with Christ comes with greater cost, cultural Christianity, which so many millions of Americans claimed when it was to their advantage, is disappearing.

Social scientists have long understood that the moral and social trajectory of a society is set by the desire to accumulate social capital. Social capital is represented by the respect, esteem, and social advancement that come to an individual or a group because they are admired and emulated within the larger society. Social capital comes to an individual by gaining credentials, personal respect, and a network of social relationships, as well as when that individual reinforces the progress of the larger society and identifies with the trajectory of the culture. For a long time, evangelical Christians held great social capital, as did those who identified with us.

There was a time when joining the First Baptist Church or the First Methodist Church garnered social capital within the community. Now, identifying with an evangelical congregation may come at the cost of a job opportunity, membership within respected social circles, and the opportunity for a voice in the public square. If an older generation of Christians acutely feels this problem, just imagine the impact this has in the lives of young evangelicals. They now arrive on the American university campus (or the high school campus for that matter) and risk social capital every time they identify themselves as evangelical Christians.

In that context, to articulate any moral judgment consistent with the Bible's declaration concerning homosexual behavior is to risk being ostracized—even in the heart of the Bible Belt. Believing and defending the Christian church's historic teaching on homosexuality in suburban Atlanta may now be almost as costly as trying to do the same in downtown Manhattan. Almost overnight, an entire world has changed.

The Church and the Sexual Revolution: Retrospect and Prospect

While we must affirm the responsibility of every individual Christian to remain faithful in times of theological crisis, an individualistic approach to the challenge of the sexual revolution is inadequate and doomed to fail. Our concern should not be limited to the individual Christian's response but must include the unified response of the believing and faithful church of the Lord Jesus Christ. The New Testament does not envision a Christian outside of the confessing and worshipping community of the church. Thus, as we consider our Christian responsibility in the face of these seismic social changes and moral challenges, our response must be grounded in Holy Scripture and in the faith "once for all delivered to the saints" (Jude 1:3)—a response that is faithful to the teachings of the apostles, to the fathers of the church, to the Reformers, and to faithful Christians throughout the centuries.

When facing a revolutionary challenge like the sexual liberation movement, Christians must recognize that our responsibility is not merely to speak for the church now, but to speak on behalf of the church historic and everlasting. We must consider those brothers and sisters who came before us and give them a voice in today's theological formulation. We must also look to Christian generations yet to come. Our response to this challenge will have much to do with whether the churches and denominations they know have any continuing fidelity to the gospel of the Lord Jesus Christ and the authority of Scripture.

We must also respond to this with the understanding that we are not led by our own wisdom. Instead, we affirm the responsibility of Christians in every generation and in every true and rightly ordered church to be directed by the Holy Spirit through the ministry of the Word.

These affirmations ground us in the Christian faith as it has been rightly preached, taught, and believed throughout millenia. These affirmations rightly ground us in the *Sensus Fidelium* of historic, biblical Christianity and bind us within the teachings of Scripture—unable to escape from Scripture as both authoritative revelation and God's gracious gift. In faithfulness to Christ, we bind ourselves to Scripture. In doing so, we seek both to live our own lives and to speak into the lives of others on the basis of the redemptive message of salvation.

Staying the Course in the Compassion of Truth

This brings us to the first issue. The church is now tempted, more than ever before in recent history, to accommodate to the new morality.

Under the watchful eye and demanding gaze of the moral revolutionaries, the church is now tempted to declare that same-sex behaviors are not sin and that the moral precepts of the gay liberation movement should be welcomed and celebrated as advances in an arc of progressive human morality.

The first problem with this is that we know that claim to be untrue. Since Scripture is the very word of God, it never fails, it never errs, and it is sufficient to reveal to us God's pattern for humanity, the truth about ourselves, and the reality of our sinfulness. To accommodate to the moral revolution and affirm its morality is to look at what the Bible calls sin and call it something else. More than that, the moral revolutionaries now demand us to shift our understanding of same-sex behaviors and relationships from the category of sin to the category of moral good. But we need to recognize and take into account what this would mean.

Such a shift would mean turning from the authority of Scripture to a new authority—the authority of the new morality. Moreover, it would mean declaring to our friends and neighbors that their sin is not actually sin. It would mean disregarding their need for a Savior.

This is where we Christians must keep our biblical and theological sanity, even when the voices around us demand we join the moral insanity. A failure on this count will not merely consign the church to lose biblical faithfulness in its voice and message—it will consign the church to mislead millions of people about their need for Jesus. Rejecting or reducing the sinfulness of sin slanders the cross of the Lord Jesus Christ. According to Scripture, Christ died for our sins. To take what Scripture declares as sin—sin for which Christ died—and to downplay its severity insults the cross of Christ and misleads sinners about their need for the salvation only available in Christ's atonement. A failure of this scale is impossible to estimate or measure.

When it is demanded that Christians respond with compassion at the expense of truth, we must understand that any compassion severed from truth is false compassion and a lie against the truth. Scripture teaches that the truth is itself compassionate. The apostle Paul spoke of this in Romans 7 when he explained how the law revealed his sin so that he understood his sin by the indictment of the moral law. "It [the law] killed me," Paul testified (Rom. 7:11), and yet he insisted that the law is good precisely because it informed him of his need for repentance and faith in the Lord Jesus Christ. In the same way, Christians must affirm the compassion of truth in this troubled generation.

The Failure of Moralism

This does not mean that the church cannot sin in truth telling. As the church considers the challenge of the present age, we must acknowledge our own sin, even when we speak the truth. Christians do not hurl the truth like a spear at a sinful world. We are called to live the truth, to teach the truth, to be the truth, and to love our neighbors on the basis of that truth. And we must admit that the church often fails at this task—and fails miserably.

As a committed evangelical Christian, I have endeavored to be faithful to Scripture and have devoted my life to understanding and teaching the truth of God as comprehensively revealed in Scripture in order to help Christians become more faithful disciples of the Lord Jesus Christ. To that end, I have regularly taught and preached on these crucial issues for several decades. Thankfully, I am confident there is no major point of teaching I now feel the need to retract. Nevertheless, I can see failings in my own life and ministry and in the larger church that are all too apparent in light of our current challenge.

The biggest problem we face is that the church far too often confuses moralism with the gospel. Moralism is one of the greatest enemies of the gospel. It represents the false hope of salvation through right behavior and moral reformation rather than by repentance and faith in the Lord Jesus Christ. As the New Testament makes explicitly clear, the church

139

has always been tempted by the dangers of moralism. Sadly, moralism often comes as a first reflex for American evangelicals. This is a truly tragic fact. Evangelicals, after all, are those who named themselves after the gospel—the *evangel*—and are supposed to be the spiritual heirs of the Reformation doctrine that salvation is all of grace.

To make the problem of moralism clear, just consider how many evangelicals would be quite happy for the homosexual challenge simply to go away. Many evangelicals, particularly older ones, would be satisfied to see America return to the society we knew in the 1950s and '60s when homosexuality was still the love "that dared not speak its name."[2] Moralism deludes us into believing that sin is no longer our problem or our responsibility when sin disappears from the cultural awareness.

In the culture in which I was raised, most middle-class Christians divided humanity between those who were "raised right" and those who were not. But hell will be filled with countless souls who were "raised right" yet died without Christ. Even for those who know that moralism is a false gospel, its spiritual instincts are always ready to creep right back into our hearts and into our moral reasoning.

The Failure of Aberrant Theology

The church's response to this challenge with the compassion of truth means we must check our claim on moral superiority at the door. Rather than acting sanctimoniously, we must be thankful that, by God's grace, Christian and biblical influences transformed the trajectory of our lives rather than the influences of the new moral authorities that would have driven us away from Scripture. If salvation really is all of grace, then our obedience to God's moral law is likewise a matter of grace. This is not to minimize the reality of sin, but rather, in every way, to remind ourselves that our own sin is just as heinous, just as horrifying, and just as deadly as homosexual sin.

We must also recognize that we have sinned against homosexuals by speaking carelessly about the true nature of their sin. I indict myself here. As mentioned in an earlier chapter, as a young theologian I was invited to speak at a conference of evangelical leaders and thinkers as the movement toward gay liberation was first taking organized shape. At that time, evangelicals were sure the element of *choice* was the central issue behind the sinfulness of homosexuality and the homosexual lifestyle. Thus, we felt the moral and theological obligation to deny the notion of a homosexual "orientation" and to insist that homosexuality was, in every case, freely chosen without regard to any predisposition. For this, I must apologize to the homosexual community, including a host of Christians who have struggled to be biblically faithful even as they have struggled with same-sex orientation.

In a fallen world, every single human being who has achieved puberty is a sexual sinner. Every single one of us has a pattern of sexual attraction, arousal, and interest that we cannot truly say we ourselves have chosen. Eventually, erotic interest comes into our awareness, and, as most adolescents can testify, it comes without any warning or explanation. I now know that a more mature, faithful, and consistent biblical understanding of human sexuality affirms that the fall has so impacted human existence that every single one of us has, to one degree or another, a fallen sexual orientation. Most Christians testify that their fallen sexual orientation is directed toward the opposite sex. Still, no Christian with a heterosexual pattern of sexual interest is free from sin or free from uninvited erotic impulses, interests, and thoughts.

Nevertheless, these uninvited thoughts do not acquit us. The Bible makes clear that we are *always* responsible for our sinful acts, even condemning us for our sinful thoughts. This is exactly what Jesus did in the Sermon on the Mount, moving beyond the Old Testament's declaration that adultery is sin to condemn even lust as adultery already committed in the heart. We are not, therefore, minimizing our accountability for our sinful acts and for the allowance of sinful thoughts. We sin against homosexuals when we minimize their personal responsibility for sexual sin and misrepresent their particular pattern of sexual interest as something they have chosen freely and can thus freely surrender.

The Christian doctrine of sin, taken with full weight and seriousness, should prevent us from believing that surrender could ever be so simple. The devastating effects of sin cling to us even as we try to separate ourselves from it. For any sinner, whether of a heterosexual or homosexual orientation, salvation and freedom are only found in Christ. Furthermore, the Bible presents the Christian life, not in terms of an instantaneous liberation from sinful impulses, but rather as an enduring discipleship—a regular, disciplined life among other Christians in the school of Christ. Repentance from sin and progressive sanctification come to believers as the Holy Spirit applies the Word of God to their hearts and conforms them to the image of Christ. Every single believer is thus a work in progress. Every movement toward obedience and conformity to Christ's image is yet another demonstration of grace at work in the life of the Christian. Once again, a robust biblical theology should inform us to expect that those struggling with same-sex attraction who come to faith in Christ and repent of their sins will continue to struggle with some of those sins and impulses until Christ calls them home.

The Failure of Isolation

The church has also sinned against gay men, lesbians, and transgendered persons by speaking of them as abstract creatures outside the lives of our own families and churches. We have spoken regularly of *them* as if they are *out there*, but those who struggle with same-sex orientation are *in here* and among us. A review of much evangelical literature during the last several decades reveals the extent to which, I am ashamed to say, evangelicals have often addressed these persons as if speaking about a tribe that inhabited a far-off island from which we can keep a safe distance. That assumption was untrue then, and it is profoundly untrue now. The church's failure on this is particularly costly, because it alienates believers who are seeking to be faithful to Christ and speaks of them as if they are a problem to be solved rather than brothers and sisters to be welcomed.

These men and women are our brothers and sisters, insofar as they are fellow repenting believers in the Lord Jesus Christ, baptized into faith and obedience, and experiencing the sanctifying ministry of the Holy Spirit. The dismissal of homosexuals and others within the sexual liberation movement as those who are "out there" also means that we have failed—often tragically—to reach out to our neighbors with true love, compassion, and the gospel of Jesus Christ.

The reason why so many of our churches look just like us is because *we prefer to be with people who are just like us.* Our idolatrous pursuit of comfort (and often our reflexive moralism) leads us to associate with people who share our moral presuppositions and our own moral and theological sentiments. Yet Christ did not command Christians to remain within a zone of cultural and moral comfort. He commanded them to go into Jerusalem and Judea and Samaria and into the uttermost parts of the world (Acts 1:8).

The New Testament itself records that the apostle Paul's love for the gospel drove him and other early believers into cities known for their lasciviousness, lust, and idolatry. In those cities, Paul did not accommodate the Christian message for the moral norm. He never minimized the sinfulness of sin, and he never insulted the cross of Christ by selling out the gospel. Paul obeyed the command. He went into the heart of cultural centers and preached the gospel.

In our modern context, the church must overcome some of the reflexes it has absorbed from cultural Christianity and "Christian" moralism. When we go to a Little League game in order to see our own children or grandchildren play and see a lesbian couple cheering on their son, we need to overcome the isolationist instinct to stay away from that couple. To the contrary, we need to sit alongside them, thankful that we have the unearned opportunity to establish a friendship and a relationship with people we know need the gospel of Jesus Christ—the same gospel we need.

This means that we must continually test and check our moral intuitions, sentiments, and reflexes over against the clear teachings of Scripture. Friendship with a person does not minimize the sinfulness of his or her sin or compromise the cross. Christian faithfulness in our generation demands that we allow ourselves to genuinely love people even when we cannot endorse their lifestyle, grant recognition to the relationship they believe they deserve, or sanction their sin. Both love and truth are essential as we establish a right relationship with our neighbors in a way that consists with our ultimate commitment to the gospel of the Lord Jesus Christ.

The Failure of Inadequate Ministry

Evangelicals have also sinned against homosexuals by failing to grapple with what authentic Christian ministry to their community should look like in the life of the church. To be honest, homosexuality has scared so many evangelicals that they would not know what to do if a person living a homosexual lifestyle showed up at the front door and urgently asked, "How can I become a Christian?" The church that fails to welcome the opportunity to answer that question is a church that fails the gospel.

The answer to that question must be the same that we would offer to any sinner—repent and believe in the Lord Jesus Christ and be saved. Of course, the answer to "what do I do now?" extends beyond the confession of faith, and far beyond the public profession of faith in baptism. It involves entering into a life of obedience and into a walk with Christ— the kind of walk that requires the church, as the communion of saints, to be a hospital for broken people who are seeking healing and wholeness in Christ. If we fail to deliver that entire message, to all people and at all times, we fail in the foremost task and responsibility of the Christian church.

We must also recognize that one of the central temptations of the present moment is to fail in exactly the opposite direction—the failure to speak the truth about the sinfulness of sin and the Bible's clear teachings on human sexuality to a generation ready to reject the Bible's message at every point. Churches starve their congregations if they do not continually feed and nourish them with the authentic preaching of the Word of God. Pastors who fail to teach the whole counsel of God will give an answer for their failure to teach Christians what must be known for faithful discipleship in the Lord Jesus. In far too many churches, Christians only learn generic truths about Christianity. This type of knowledge cannot offer any robust intellectual or theological defense of the scriptural teachings on gender, sex, marriage, and morality.

The Failure of Shallow Youth Discipleship

Finally, the church has often failed young Christians. We have failed to form them in the faith, to ground them in truth, and to prepare them for discipleship in a post-Christian age. Recent studies of Christian adolescents and young adults point to the fact that, in the main, their understanding of Christianity is actually what sociologist Christian Smith identified as "moralistic therapeutic deism."[3] Teenagers and young adults believe that there is indeed a God. Yet their understanding of God is basically deistic. They believe there is a creator but that he has removed himself from the activity of the world and, though basically positively inclined toward his creatures, is not actively involved in their lives.

These young people are also moralistic. They believe there is an authoritative and ultimate moral law to which we are all accountable but that the moral code of tolerance and acceptance as defined by modern secular elites is essentially good. These young people are also committed to a therapeutic understanding of religion, believing that the end result of any good thing, including religious faith, must be that people will feel better about themselves, be happy, and overcome any "hang-ups" they may have inherited from the past.

Christian Smith and his research team define moralistic therapeutic deism as essentially coming down to this creed:

1. A God exists who created and orders the world and watches over human life on earth.
2. God wants people to be good, nice, and fair to each other, as taught in the Bible and by most world religions.
3. The central goal of life is to be happy and to feel good about oneself.
4. God does not need to be particularly involved in one's life except when God is needed to resolve a problem.
5. Good people go to heaven when they die.[4]

Of course, this is not biblical Christianity in any recognizable form—yet far too many youth in our churches believe it to be. As Smith and his colleagues continued their research on these same teenagers when they moved into "emerging adulthood," they found that moralistic therapeutic deism extended into the next decade of their lives. Smith explained, "most emerging adults are happy with religion so long as it is general and accepting of diversity but are uncomfortable if it is anything else."[5] Sadly, many of the teenagers and young adults described in this research were raised in evangelical churches and homes. They almost surely heard at least some teaching from the Bible on questions of sexuality and morality. But, what they received was so insubstantial, so disconnected from the larger metanarrative of Scripture, and so devoid of serious moral and intellectual content that it evaporated as soon as they encountered a peer culture more committed to tolerance than any other moral principle.

In recent years, we have been warned regularly that the millennial generation is increasingly hostile to biblical Christianity, specifically accusing conservative Christians of being intolerant on issues of human sexuality. In their book *unChristian: What a New Generation Really Thinks about Christianity*, David Kinnaman and Gabe Lyons explained, "The gay issue has become the 'big one,' the negative image most likely to be intertwined with Christianity's reputation. It is also the dimension that most clearly demonstrates the unChristian faith to young people today, surfacing a spate of negative perceptions: judgmental, bigoted, sheltered, right-wingers, hypocritical, insincere, and uncaring."[6] In a massive survey of young adults, Kinnaman and Lyons found that the millennials identified a posture of judgment against homosexuality to be the number one reason millennials rejected or abandoned Christianity.

In a second project, Kinnaman looked at the lives of young people *inside* the church and found a similar pattern. So many of these church-going young people expressed the concern that Christianity was simply too judgmental, especially on issues of sexual morality—homosexuality in particular. As Kinnaman explained, "The ages eighteen to twenty-nine are the black hole of church attendance; this age is 'missing in action' for most congregations." The "missing in action" often point to what they describe as the exclusionary intolerant posture of the church as the reason for their absence.[7]

It simply will not serve the church to deny that we face a massive challenge communicating the truth of the Bible and the power of the gospel to this generation. Granted, the church is not fully responsible for this predicament. While it is true that the church has often failed both to teach faithfully and to speak lovingly, the fact is that the church finds itself now in alien territory in a post-Christian culture. This points to the fact that too many young Christians, or, at the very least, too many young people who have been within our churches, simply have no adequate notion of Christian truth and discipleship. They have been entertained, coddled, and cajoled, but they have not been mentored, and they have not been disciplined and loved by the Christian community.

We cannot possibly expect a generation of young Christians to be faithful if they see themselves as doing nothing more than parroting simplistic moral principles given to them by their parents and pastors. They will move into faithfulness only if they are grounded in the fabric of the faith and in the deep truths of Christianity. They will continue in faithfulness only if they see themselves standing in continuity with a Christian community rooted in the apostolic age.

Contrary to appearances, I know that the millennial generation is not lost to the church, and that this largest generation in American history holds massive promise for the church and for gospel ministry. As the president of a seminary and a college, it is my great privilege to look at thousands of faithful young people pushing back against the culture and standing for the Christian faith. They have not come to seminary and college looking for a minimalistic, moralistic, superficial, cultural Christianity. They come because they want to be counted faithful in the long line of gospel ministers that stretches from the book of Acts to the coffee shops, neighborhoods, campuses, and megacities of our own day.

The choice before the church is clear: we will either ground this generation in the grandeur and glory of all that biblical Christianity represents, or we will see the roster of the "missing in action" grow to even more tragic proportions. Seen in this light, the challenge of the sexual revolution serves as a catalyst to call the church to wake up from a moral slumber into a life of bold and authentic Christian witness and faithful living.

Reformation or Retreat

In light of the immensity of the challenge, some Christian leaders are rightly reminding the church of the New Testament's teaching that we are an "exilic" people.[8] As a historian and theologian, I submit that the church has often been most faithful during times of exile and cultural marginalization. We must now repent that we ever constituted a "moral majority." The confessing church is always a moral minority. Those who seemed to share our morality in times past, without sharing our theology, were quick to exchange their own moral understanding when the morality of the culture changed around them. The collapse of cultural Christianity was not the collapse of the Christian church—merely the collapse of those who were living off of the social capital of Christianity.

The New Testament has always witnessed to the fact that Christians would be exiles and strangers. The apostle Peter referred to believers as "elect exiles of the Dispersion" (1 Peter 1:1)—affirming that exile has been the experience of believers from the very beginning of the Christian church.

Yet exile does not mean an end to Christian witness or to Christian faithfulness. Peter also commanded Christians to be witnesses to the salvation that is found in Christ and to live as obedient children. In a most memorable passage, Peter described the church as "a chosen race, a royal priesthood, a holy nation, a people for his own possession, that you may proclaim the excellencies of him who called you out of darkness into his marvelous light" (1 Peter 2:9). But Peter also instructed the church "to abstain from the passions of the flesh, which wage war against your soul" and to "keep your conduct among the Gentiles honorable, so that when they speak against you as evildoers, they may see your good deeds and glorify God on the day of visitation" (vv. 11–12). This is precisely where the faithful Christian church finds itself today.

We are called to be Christ's people, a people who bear evidence of the power of the gospel in our lives and demonstrate obedience through faithfulness to Christ and bold Christian witness. But we are also called to watch our own conduct, maintaining honorable lives so that even when we are slandered by the world, that very slander bears testimony to our faithfulness.

America's post-Christian culture is filled with people who believe that they have heard too much from the Christian church—too much judgment, too much moralism, too much intolerance. The New Testament, however, tells us that the world around us has seen and heard far too little of authentic Christianity.

It is simply natural that we would think and worry about our own status within the larger culture. Exile is always hard and often excruciating. Nevertheless, the hardening of the culture toward Christian morality must not dissuade us from boldness in communicating Christian truth. The temptation to withdraw is a temptation to unfaithfulness. We must stand our ground.

Christians in obedience to Christ cannot quit seeking a society that leads to human flourishing. Christians committed to the Bible cannot believe that human flourishing can come at the expense of recognizing marriage as the union of a man and a woman, or at the expense of recognizing sex as God's gift to be directed by his sovereign plan. Love of neighbor compels us to be involved in the cultural conversation and in the struggle to protect the most basic institution of civilization—the monogamous, covenantal union of a man and a woman. We must continue to bear witness to marriage not only in our teaching but in our marriages.

Finally, we must continue to teach everything the Bible teaches about sex, sexuality, gender, and self-identity, refusing to surrender to the spirit of the age in order to escape exile. Carl F. H. Henry encouraged his generation of evangelicals to avoid any surrender of cultural and moral responsibility by volunteering to be "a wilderness cult in a secular society with no more public significance than the ancient Essenes in their Dead Sea caves."[9]

We must not exile ourselves, and we certainly must not retreat into silence while we still have a platform, a voice, and an opportunity. We must remind ourselves again and again of the compassion of truth and the truth of compassion. We must look in the mirror and recognize that when we speak to others, we are speaking as sinners saved by grace. We must say all that we know on the basis of all that Scripture reveals and trust that only God can make that message convincing and compelling to our audience.

We must worship faithfully in our churches and glorify God for the goodness of his creation. We must remain faithful to our own marital commitments and demonstrate marital love and fidelity. We must raise our children in the nurture and admonition of the Lord, and ground the rising generation in the truths of God's Word, the power of the gospel, and the glory of Christian faithfulness. Finally, Christians must look each other in the eye and remind one another of what is now required of us—to speak the truth, to live the truth, and to bear witness to the truth whether we are invited to the White House or treated as exiles. The rest is in God's hands.

10

THE HARD QUESTIONS

Question 1: Aren't Christians being selective with Old Testament law when they appeal to it with respect to homosexuality, while ignoring Old Testament commands about clothing, food, etc.?

In some sense, yes, because we are singling out the moral law, which is exactly what the New Testament trains us to do. The book of Acts distinctly separates the ceremonial and liturgical laws from the moral law. The Lord told Peter not to distinguish between clean and unclean animals any longer (Acts 10:9–16). At the same time, the Jerusalem Council clearly confirmed the continuation of the moral law (Acts 15). Paul tells us the gospel is for the Gentiles as well as for the Jews, which obliterates that distinction in the holiness code. Nevertheless, Paul regularly returns to the moral law of the Old Testament to show and defend the character of righteous living in general and the commandments against same-sex acts in particular.

If we still depended on the Levitical code for our understanding of sex, the church would have an incomplete picture of human sexuality. Thankfully, Scripture provides us with a comprehensive picture of this issue in the New Testament. As a result, the church's basic understanding of the sinfulness of homosexual acts is not finally rooted in Leviticus; it is rooted in the New Testament, and specifically in texts like Romans 1. The consistent identification of all same-sex acts as explicitly sinful reveals the unquestionable continuity between the Old and New Testaments.

Question 2: Since Jesus did not specifically address homosexuality, how can we be certain he considers it sinful behavior?

Jesus addressed a multitude of sins throughout the four Gospels. As evidenced in the Sermon on the Mount, he explicitly affirmed the continuation of the Old Testament moral law and its intensification in his kingdom. At the same time, there are many specific issues, both ancient and modern, for which there is no specific scriptural text explicitly revealing what Christ said during his earthly ministry. This does not mean we cannot know what Christ believed and taught.

In answering a question about divorce, Jesus himself stated that God's plan from the beginning was that a man and a woman be united in marriage. Jesus affirmed the Genesis pattern of complementarity, and he honored the institution of marriage as the conjugal union of a man and a woman (Mark 10:2–9). At every single point, Jesus affirmed the Old Testament's judgment against sexual sin. Moreover, he pushed the point even deeper by moving from the Old Testament's prohibition of the external act to an even bigger concern—the sinful nature of the human heart.

Question 3: Some scholars have asserted that Paul's writings about homosexuality are actually about abusive homosexual relationships (i.e., rape, prostitution, etc.). Isn't it the case that what Paul says does not apply to consensual same-sex relationships?

Due to the work of Robert Gagnon and many other biblical scholars, we know that this was not the case.[1] Secular historians of the Roman Empire also record clear examples of consensual, adult same-sex relationships in the Greco-Roman world. Paul knew exactly what he was condemning.

Christians need to remember, given the doctrine of the divine inspiration of Scripture, that when Paul condemns something, the Holy Spirit condemns it as well. When we cite Paul, we cite the Holy Spirit.

Romans 1 and 1 Corinthians 5 present a very sophisticated argument for the sinfulness of same-sex acts and same-sex relationships. In 1 Corinthians 5, Paul demonstrates an undeniable belief in the sinfulness of both the passive and the active participants involved in the act of male same-sex intercourse. This is stunning given that the secular view in the ancient world only viewed the passive participant as the shameful one. In the ancient world, the passive partner in male homosexual intercourse was shameful in taking the role of a woman, but the active partner continued to act in an essentially masculine way. Paul, on the other hand, by grounding his argument in Leviticus 18, demonstrated that both partners were engaged in a sinful act and under the threat of divine condemnation.

Question 4: The biblical authors did not have the category of orientation, so aren't they talking about something different than we are?

If sexual orientation refers to a pattern of sexual interest and arousal, then the Bible is actually quite explicit about this. In Romans 1, for example, Paul addressed not only men who have unnatural relations with men and women who have unnatural relations with women, but also those who burn with same-sex passions toward one another. This language reflects sexual preference and a pattern of sexual arousal that corresponds with the modern concept of sexual orientation. Furthermore, the Bible recognizes something even more fundamental than a sexual orientation—it recognizes a sinful orientation. Scripture communicates that every single human being is born with a sinful orientation. We all have a pattern of interest, ambitions, and temptations unique to us. Further, every single human being who has experienced puberty has a sexual orientation that, in some way, falls short of the glory of God.

Question 5: Is homosexual sin worse than other sins?

It is very tempting to suggest that all sins are equally sinful. In some sense, every single sin sufficiently justifies our eternal damnation and separation from an infinitely holy and righteous God. Yet not all sins are equal in ambition, context, or effect. They are not all equal in ambition because some sins are so deeply rooted in conscious rebellion that they amount to blatant disobedience or refusal to believe. With regard to context, the Bible itself distinguishes sin. Some are described as "against nature" and others are not. Paul did this in Romans 1 when he spoke about homosexuality. He used the same argument in 1 Corinthians 6 when he showed that sexual sin has a particularly sinful quality since it is, unlike other sins, directed against the body, which he argued is a temple of the Holy Spirit. Even in the Old Testament, some sins are referred to as abominations, which effectively set them apart from other sins.[2]

Nor is all sin equal in effect. Some sins cause physical death. Others cause far less immediate and apparent consequences. For this reason, even the criminal justice system recognizes different levels of criminality and assigns different penalties for different criminal acts. The Old and New Testaments make the same distinction. Nevertheless, every single sin is opposed to the infinite justice and righteousness of God and thus deserving of God's righteous punishment.

Question 6: Are people born gay? Doesn't this mean God made them gay?

No adequate scientific evidence exists that suggests an individual can be "born" with a same-sex sexual orientation. Nevertheless, the testimony of those struggling with same-sex attraction reveals that that attraction and sense of sexual interest can come very early. Indeed, it can come so early that many people cannot pinpoint how early such an interest appeared.

Christians should not run from this question. Biblical theology reminds us that the consequences of the fall are so comprehensive that we should expect sin to impact everything from our self-centeredness to molecular structure. If a biological cause or genetic link explaining same-sex attraction is ever discovered, Christians should be among the least surprised. Such a finding would certainly inform our pastoral understanding and approach to persons with a same-sex orientation because we recognize that sin even affects our biology. Such a discovery would reveal what will likely be a lifelong struggle of sexual interest and personal identity, even for someone who knows Christ as Savior and seeks to live in holiness before him.

That being said, an analysis of the current data reveals no adequate scientific evidence for a "gay" gene.[3] Furthermore, most geneticists believe that something as complicated as sexual orientation is not likely to be simply traced to a single gene. That is simply far too simplistic an understanding of human genetics.

Christians must remember that we live in a culture in which people instinctively ascribe authority to reports trumpeting a scientific discovery. This often leads to a change in moral judgment, even when that report is not replicated by other scientists or is later withdrawn.

Christians should not be surprised if the day comes when the preponderance of evidence suggests some biological pattern of causality. The discovery of a "gay gene" would not force the church to abandon its position on the sinfulness of homosexuality, nor would it nullify the clear teaching of Scripture or validate same-sex attraction. As those informed by Scripture, Christians must constantly remember that the natural world we now experience is a natural world tainted by human sin and under God's judgment. This is why we depend on Scripture to understand God's pattern for human flourishing, and trust what it says about the morality of same-sex acts rather than what a scientific journal says.

Question 7: More and more evangelicals are embracing same-sex unions. Isn't this an issue where we can agree to disagree? If not, why?

We can "agree to disagree" in the sense that the issue is likely destined to be one of lasting disagreement. If we are committed to Scripture, human flourishing, the gospel, and love of neighbor, however, then an issue of this magnitude compels us to plead with and attempt to persuade those who will face the eternal wrath of God if they do not abandon their sin for Jesus. Our greatest responsibility is to point sinners to the cross of Christ and the promise of salvation for all who believe.

Those with common sense on both sides of the issue reject the suggestion that there can be a third way or that some kind of neutral ground can be reached. There are many issues—same-sex marriage and homosexuality central among them—on which the answer eventually must be a yes or no. Every single church must eventually accept or reject the legitimacy of same-sex marriage. Every congregation, Christian institution, and religious organization will eventually have to make a decision on the issue of homosexuality. There is no integrity in the resignation to simply "agree to disagree" on an issue in which the gospel and the authority of Scripture—and ultimately the eternal state of human beings—are at stake.

Question 8: If the church cannot come to a consensus on this issue, doesn't that mean the Bible is not clear?

To answer this question, we have to go all the way back to the Reformation. One of the great affirmations about Scripture made by the Reformers is what is known as the *perspicuity* of Scripture, which is another way of talking about the *clarity* of Scripture. Scripture continually speaks in such a manner that clarifies issues, not obscures them.

The reality in a sinful world is that our understanding is often unclear even where Scripture is clear. The Reformers pointed to the clarity of Scripture in order to affirm that any Christian who opened the Bible heard the word of God and faced the decision to obey or disobey.

That was true when the church received the New Testament and when the Reformers asserted the principle, and it remains true now. If people who affirm the truthfulness of Scripture cannot come to a consensus on this issue, the problem is not in Scripture—it is in a failure to rightly understand and obey it.

Question 9: Since the sexual revolution uses the rhetoric of the civil rights movement, should we differentiate between racial identity and sexual identity?

In response to this question, Christians must engage carefully in the task of biblical theology. The diversity of races and ethnicities comprises part of God's plan (see, for example, the table of nations in Genesis 10). The Bible also indicates that God is pleased that his human creatures are organized by families, clans, languages, and nations. Furthermore, Revelation 5 indicates that this pleasure is an eternal pleasure for God. Those gathered around the Lamb's throne are men and women from every tongue, tribe, and nation who have all been ransomed by Christ. Thus, Scripture celebrates racial differences. The Bible celebrates these distinctions as part of God's glorious diversity in creation.

The Bible, however, unquestionably expresses *only one* legitimate pattern of human sexuality. Only one framework exists in which conjugal acts can be enjoyed and celebrated—the monogamous, faithful marriage of a man and a woman. The Bible consistently declares anything outside of this framework as sin. Christians, therefore, must think carefully on this issue. Even though we accept that certain individuals have different sexual orientations, we do not accept sexual orientation as synonymous with race or ethnicity. We recognize racism as sin because it denies and subverts our common descent from Adam and Eve and our common origin in the will of the Creator. We do not celebrate diversity of sexual "orientations" because the Bible does not allow it.

In matters of the law, this issue is often framed in terms of "mutable" and "immutable" characteristics. For Christians, however, these terms do not go far enough. This issue is not simply a matter of parsing out what is "mutable" and "immutable" in a person's character. Instead, as Christians, we must return to the theological foundation provided for us in the doctrine of creation. We must ask ourselves one question: Was this part of God's original plan and purpose for his human creatures?

Question 10: What is a theologically faithful definition of sexual orientation? Does sexual orientation affect one's sexual identity?

Christians must be honest enough to recognize that the modern secular understanding of sexual orientation has legitimate insights that we can appropriate in a way consistent with evangelical theology, Scripture, and the Christian tradition. Christians in general, and evangelicals in particular, must admit that we have often had a very superficial understanding of sexuality. We assumed for centuries that people simply chose their pattern of sexual interest. The modern secular concept of sexual orientation suggests that every single human being who has reached the age of sexual maturity is characterized by a specific pattern of sexual interest that includes sexual arousal, sexual fantasy, sexual expectation, and a hope for specific sexual fulfillment.

From the vantage point of biblical theology and orthodox pastoral counsel, the modern notion of sexual orientation helps us see how deeply situated matters of sexual interest, sexual arousal, and sexual fulfillment really are in our lives. If these matters are so embedded in our lives, we must recognize the sinful and harmful superficiality in telling those who struggle with same-sex orientation to just simply stop being attracted to someone of the same gender. Nevertheless, this does not mean we are allowed to resign ourselves to whatever sexual orientation and pattern of arousal we discover in ourselves. Rather, as children of God, we must submit ourselves in every respect, including our sexual identities and orientations, to God. This submission is an act of obedience that leads to human flourishing.

Sexual orientation first became a public issue because those pushing for the normalization of homosexuality argued that sexual orientation simply had to be accepted at face value as normal and natural. That, however, is simply not the case. While we should understand the legitimate insights the concept of sexual orientation offers, we should also remember that a disordered sexual orientation reveals the sinfulness of sin. It is important to note that sexual orientation often reflects our sinful orientation. Some are more tempted to dishonesty, others to temptations of pride, others to temptations of greed, and others to temptations of lust. The reality of a sinful orientation does not reduce or nullify the distorted nature of that orientation—not in the slightest.

Question 11: Is experiencing same-sex attraction itself sinful? Do Christians who experience same-sex attraction need to repent of their orientation, or only of homosexual action and lust?

First, this is not a question limited to issues of sexuality in general, or sexual acts and sexual orientation in particular. This question relates to the larger theological question of temptation and behavior. Every child growing into maturity recognizes the distinction between the temptation and the act. Every criminal law system also understands the difference between the temptation and the act. Rather than imprisoning people for every criminal temptation, the law distinguishes between the temptation of a criminal act and the performance of a criminal act. Every parent understands that same distinction when raising children and when they look in the mirror. Therefore, Christians must distinguish between temptation and the performance of sin.

Still, there is indeed something sinful about being tempted to rob a bank. Obviously, it is less sinful than robbing a bank. And its consequence and the effects are certainly quite different. We would be right to say, "Even if you have the temptation, don't perform the act," but we would be wrong to say, "The temptation is not an issue of sinful consequence."

We tend to assume that an uninvited temptation is something for which we are not accountable. But no one knows himself well enough to fully understand where our temptations come from or to what degree we have given ourselves over to that interest. Christians, therefore, must pray that we not be tempted, just as Jesus instructed his disciples to do in the Lord's Prayer.

Finally, we come to the issue of defining sexual orientation. Sexual orientation is a pattern of temptation. Again, we must stress this is not the only pattern of sexual sin. Heterosexual sinners are tempted to lust toward someone of the opposite sex. Married persons are tempted to lust for someone who is not their spouse. A person who has a pattern of same-sex attraction is tempted in a similar manner. Same-sex orientation, however, cannot be channeled into a legitimate sexual outlet, whereas a heterosexual orientation can be channeled into the faithful, monogamous institution of marriage. For this reason, same-sex orientation presents a greater struggle.

Must a Christian who struggles with same-sex attraction repent of the mere feeling of attraction, even if he does not act on that feeling or lust in his heart? Because same-sex attraction is a disordered attraction, some degree of repentance certainly needs to happen. Consider this analogous scenario. Imagine a teenage boy who has become a Christian is assigned to read a particular book in school. He is not responsible for choosing the book; the teacher, after all, assigned it to him. Something of a sexual nature is presented in the book, and he finds himself aroused and interested. He does not, however, give himself to lust. He simply moves past the explicit passage. Later, the explicit passage comes back to his mind. Once again, he refuses the temptation to lust. Nevertheless, he will almost surely feel some sense of guilt for letting thoughts resurface in the first place. Every time these thoughts come to his mind, the boy is making a moral decision, even as he wards off lustful thoughts with repentance and by grace.

Most Christians recognize sinful things that are unintentional and not premeditated regularly enter our minds. Nevertheless, these thoughts arrive, and so these thoughts produce some moral accountability, even though we seek to push them out of our fantasies and imaginations. This common experience among all Christians—indeed among all humanity—reveals that sin is more deeply rooted in our hearts than we ourselves know. This is one of the reasons repentance regularly marks the Christian life.

People struggling with same-sex attraction must understand that they are in the same position as any other sinner. We all need to live lives of constant repentance, recognizing that the entire Christian life is one of constant temptation to sin and simultaneous call to obey Christ. This, of course, does not minimize the particularly difficult challenges those who struggle with a same-sex attraction face. But these men and women should not be separated from the rest of the body of Christ into a different category of sin and sanctification. For this reason, Christians need to be candid with one another and not assume that only a few people in the congregation struggle with sin. *Every person* in the congregation struggles with sin.

Question 12: Should a Christian attend a same-sex wedding ceremony?

The simple answer is no, but, of course, there are a number of complex issues we must think about here. We can all understand just how excruciatingly difficult it will be for Christians to not attend or participate in the same-sex ceremonies of family and friends. It is tempting to think that our presence at the ceremony can be understood merely as an act of identification with the two people involved without giving moral approval to their union. But no one attends a wedding with a suspended moral judgment. And this is precisely the problem.

Attending a wedding ceremony *always* signals moral approval. This is why *The Book of Common Prayer* (which has provided the traditional ceremonial language known to millions of people throughout the centuries) contains the phrase that asks if anyone knows any cause that should prevent the marriage—"speak now; or else forever hold your peace." These words reveal the historic function of the wedding ceremony as a gathering of celebrants who come together to grant moral approval to the union of two people in marriage. Attending a same-sex marriage ceremony is to grant a positive and public moral judgment to the union. At some point, that attendance will involve congratulating the couple for their union. There will be no way to claim moral neutrality when congratulating a couple upon their wedding. If you cannot congratulate the couple, how can you attend?

Some Christians may point to the example of Jesus, who regularly ate with sinners, as warrant for attending a same-sex ceremony. While Jesus clearly did extend table fellowship to those who were publicly known to be in sin, his constant call was to repentance. In no case in the Gospels did Jesus ever allow his presence to endorse sin. Further, eating a meal with someone is not a celebration of any particular sin. When Jesus did appear at a wedding, as in the wedding of Cana in Galilee, his presence was intended to show moral approval. Attending a same-sex wedding today would send a very different signal from that set by Jesus in the Gospels.

Question 13: Should we use the term "gay"?

This question must be answered in different ways depending on the time, context, and individuals. The contemporary movement to normalize homosexuality has intentionally shifted descriptions such as "sodomy" to "homosexual" and then to "gay." Furthermore, activists now embrace words that were first used as hurtful descriptions (such as "queer") as a way of identifying their own cause. Even among those advocating the normalization of homosexuality and the legalization of same-sex marriage, there is no unanimity on the correct language. Thus, the seemingly endless series of initials—*LGBT, LGBTQQ2IA, QUILTBAG,* and so on.

For a long time, those seeking to normalize same-sex acts and relationships endorsed the term *gay*. More recently, there has been an effort to move beyond *gay* to a multitude of other possible words. Christians speaking about these issues should use language that is the most clear and least intentionally offensive. At the same time, we lose something when we use the word *gay*. This is true of any word that seeks to avoid moral clarity. Unlike other words, *homosexuality* has the advantage of speaking with sharp particularity to the actual issue at stake.

Question 14: Can a person with same-sex attraction change his or her orientation? If so, how?

At one level we must answer this question with affirmative conviction. Yes, a person with same-sex attraction can change. Christians must proclaim that rebellious sinners, whether heterosexual or homosexual, can be redeemed by Christ and conformed to his image by the Holy Spirit. We can affirm this without hesitation because of God's promises in Scripture and because of the gospel's transformative power.

At the same time, the process of sanctification and the radical change from sexual sinner to a life of purity and holiness is never simple. The redemption of someone with same-sex attraction does not instantaneously produce a heterosexual orientation. The New Testament displays the difficulty of escaping patterns of temptation and sin. In Romans 7, Paul demonstrates the tension Christians experience between new life in Christ and indwelling sin. There is simply no easy way to escape the lingering effects of our sin even after conversion to Christ. We must honestly state that it is humanly impossible to reverse our sexual orientation by force of will.

In light of this, all Christians, especially those tempted by sexual sin, must lean into the truth of justification by faith alone and a sanctification progressively worked out in us by the Holy Spirit through the ministry of the Word. Christians must trust that our bodies and sexual orientations will be fully redeemed when Christ returns and consummates his redemptive work.

Many Christians struggling with a same-sex sexual attraction indicate that the struggle is lifelong. Some have testified of great gains and some have testified of a reversal of sexual attraction, though this seems to be given to a minority of believers in this struggle. Regrettably, Christians have often sinned against those who struggle with same-sex orientation by suggesting that their patterns of sexual attraction can be easily altered. The effects of sin are so devastating, pervasive, and situated in us, however, that change is never easily accomplished.

While Christians should be thankful that Romans 7 reveals the nature of indwelling sin in the believer, we must also maintain a genuine hope about the potential for growth in godliness. The same Paul who cried out in despair, "Wretched man that I am! Who will deliver me from this body of death?" also cried out, "Thanks be to God through Jesus Christ our Lord!" (Rom. 7:24–25). Even in our body of death, we are being freed from the power of sin.

Ultimately, someone with a homosexual orientation can change. Behavior will be the first area to change. When we come to Christ, our first responsibility is to align our behavior, including our sexual acts, with the clear revelation of God in Scripture. Then, by pursuing the means of grace, the Holy Spirit can increasingly bring our sexual orientations into obedience to the Word of God. We cannot promise that this will be complete in this life, but we can be fully confident that he who began a good work in us will complete it in the end (Phil. 1:6).

Question 15: Should a pastor promote reparative therapy? If a believer is dealing with same-sex attraction, should he or she pursue reparative therapy?

The best evidence seems to show that reparative therapy works for some but not all. Unfortunately, it is very difficult to predict when this type of therapy may or may not be helpful. The evidence suggests that reparative therapy is most helpful for those who express the deepest desire for the therapy to work and for those whose same-sex behaviors were, as they themselves admit, more episodic than those who fully embraced a same-sex orientation. Forcing someone into reparative therapy, however, is likely to do more harm than good.

Christians should never expect salvation from reparative therapy, nor should we offer the promise of sanctification by any mere therapy. Salvation comes only in the gospel of Christ and sanctification only in the ministry of the Holy Spirit through the Word. Nevertheless, there are means we can use that help us grow in grace. We must make certain we never place our hope and trust in a therapeutic promise. Therapy will never save us. Only Christ can do that.

Question 16: Should Christian parents allow their children to play at the homes of children who have parents in a same-sex union?

Christians tend to swing between two problematic extremes on this issue. On the one hand, we often believe that friendship with someone forces us to deny the sinfulness of his sin. On the other hand, Christians often mistakenly believe biblical faithfulness requires us to separate from anyone involved in ongoing public sin. Neither of these options is faithful to the gospel.

Since a simple yes or no will not serve us in this situation, I propose that we remember the following truths and let them inform our worldview and ethical decisions on these matters. First, I would encourage Christians not to radically separate from our neighbors in such a way that we prohibit our children from playing with their children. Instead, we should make every effort to develop real and authentic friendships with our LGBT neighbors.

Paul tells us "not to associate with sexually immoral people" (1 Cor. 5:9). He follows up these words with, "Not at all meaning the sexually immoral of this world . . . since then you would need to go out of the world" (v. 10). The context of Paul's words shows us that he is telling us to avoid sexually immoral people *within the church*—that is, with those who claim to be a Christian brother or sister (v. 11). Paul's words provide a crucial theological model for faithful living. Christians are in the world in order to preach the gospel and to work for the good of our neighbors so that they might live more flourishing lives and follow Jesus Christ. That can only happen if we develop genuine friendships with our neighbors.

The real danger is not that we allow our children to play in the homes of same-sex couples. The real danger is that Christian parents do not teach their children a comprehensive biblical understanding of the gospel, sin, scriptural authority, and sexuality. The Christian parents who fail to disciple their children before sending them into the home of a same-sex couple (or any other part of the world for that matter) are setting their children up for theological confusion and great harm.

Question 17: Is the affirmation of the moral legitimacy of same-sex sexuality grounds for church discipline if the believer affirms the inerrancy and authority of Scripture? Isn't this just a quibble over interpretation?

An affirmation of the inerrancy of Scripture and a total commitment to the inerrancy of Scripture are not the same. Many people propositionally affirm the inerrancy of Scripture yet approach Scripture in a manner inconsistent with the conviction that the Bible is true and trustworthy in all that it reveals. Affirming biblical inerrancy is necessary, but it does not guarantee an accurate handling of the biblical text.

Paul told Timothy, "Do your best to present yourself to God as one approved, a worker who has no need to be ashamed, rightly handling the word of truth" (2 Tim. 2:15). The task of interpreting Scripture is indeed complex, but the character of Scripture provides us with a basic framework for the interpretive process: read Scripture as God speaking; interpret Scripture by other Scripture; affirm and presuppose the theological unity of Scripture; and approach Scripture with faith seeking understanding. The only way one can neutralize and subvert the clear teachings of Scripture—so clear that even the most honest advocates of the sexual revolution admit its consistent negative judgment—is by treating Scripture as something other than inerrant. Regrettably, many who claim to affirm the inerrancy of Scripture treat Scripture as if it is not.

Furthermore, we must always remember that the interpretive community of Scripture is not the individual—the interpretive community of Scripture is the believing church. This does not mean we should adopt a Roman Catholic notion of an authoritative magisterium within the church. Nor does this suggest an anointed priesthood. Instead, the New Testament points to the believing congregation as the interpretive community of Scripture. It is simply not enough to affirm the inerrancy of Scripture propositionally. One must also stand with today's faithful believers and those throughout the ages in their reading of and obedience to God's Word.

Question 18: Ancient creeds and confessions do not address marriage as a matter of Christian orthodoxy. Isn't demanding adherence to traditional marriage inconsistent with the history of the church?

Our affirmation that a traditional understanding of marriage is essential to Christian orthodoxy is only inconsistent with the history of the church in that a traditional understanding of marriage has never been challenged in the way it is today. History testifies that heresy precedes orthodoxy in formal assertion. Every ancient creed was written in response to heretical teachings. In other words, theological controversies forced the church to state clearly its convictions on pressing issues.

Thus, the fact that marriage was never addressed by any of the ancient creeds or confessions demonstrates that it never needed to be addressed because it was never a matter of controversy. Creeds are con-textual documents—theological responses to sub-orthodox teachings situated in a specific time and context. Errors are not corrected until after they arise.

That no one ever questioned the biblical and traditional understand-ing of marriage as the covenant union of a man and a woman explains why the church never addressed the issue of marriage in a creedal or con-fessional format. The church did not call councils to address problems that did not exist.

Question 19: If I am a Christian who experiences same-sex attraction, should I pray to not have homosexual feelings?

Every Christian should pray exactly as the Lord taught us to pray in the Lord's Prayer: "Thy kingdom come, Thy will be done in earth, as it is in heaven" (Matt. 6:10 KJV). This kind of prayer not only longs for world systems to align with the kingdom of Christ, but also longs for our lives to align with God's will. It reflects a desire to become more faithful to Christ and more conformed to his image. This certainly includes our sexual orientation.

We should also pray, "Lead us not into temptation, but deliver us from evil" (v. 13). Asking God to draw us away from things that tempt us should be the content of our prayer. We should ask God to replace temp-tation with holiness. Heterosexuals are also tempted sexually. "Lead us not into temptation" is a prayer for both the heterosexual Christian and the Christian battling same-sex attraction, or any other form of sexual desire.

Question 20: If I am a Christian who experiences same-sex attraction, will I become more heterosexual as I become more mature in my walk with Christ?

Some Christians in this situation will discover an increased self-understanding of heterosexual orientation. I know couples who have come together as husband and wife after one or both struggled with same-sex attraction, and who found great fulfillment and joy in the gift of heterosexual marriage and the gift of children. But this should not be the universal expectation.

Many other believers strive to be faithful to Christ and obey the Word but experience no heterosexual pattern of sexual arousal. Progressive sanctification through the Holy Spirit will come for Christians who experience same-sex attraction, but that does not mean they will become more heterosexual the more they grow in godliness. Sanctification leads us into holiness and out of sin. This is why sanctification may lead an individual with same-sex attraction into holy celibacy, rather than heterosexuality.

Question 21: What should someone who has an ongoing, seemingly unchanged pattern of same-sex attraction do in obedience to Christ?

That Christian must, by the authority of Scripture and in obedience to the gospel, submit everything she is to Christ. For someone who has an ongoing, seemingly unchanged, and perhaps unchangeable (in this life) pattern of same-sex attraction, the call to holiness would appear, in most cases, to be a call to celibacy. In all cases, it would be a call to avoid sexual sin and any celebration of a sexual orientation that disobeys God and his Word. No escape from same-sex attraction may come. Thus, celibacy, honored by Christ himself and regarded by the apostle Paul, would appear to be the requirement of faithfulness and obedience.

The Christian church has failed in not affirming the gift of celibacy. It has failed to show how the gift of celibacy reflects obedience to Christ and the glory of God. The Christian church has also failed to honor those who give themselves to lives of celibacy for the sake of the gospel, a lifestyle Paul commended for its advantages (1 Cor. 7:25–40). Celibacy allows a person to do things for Christ's kingdom that a married person simply will not get to do.

Christians must embrace sexual renunciation for the sake of Christ. *All* Christians are called to sexual renunciation for at least some time. For heterosexual believers, this means voluntary sexual renunciation until marriage and a renunciation of all sex outside of marriage. For those with same-sex orientation, this means sexual renunciation for a lifetime. Jesus himself honored those who, for his sake, made themselves "eunuchs for the sake of the kingdom of heaven" (Matt. 19:12).

For those for whom marriage would not remedy sin, celibacy is the only other option, and the church should honor it just as it honors marriage. It is, in so many cases, a considerable sacrifice. We should take Jesus seriously when he speaks of honoring those who become eunuchs for the sake of the kingdom. That shocking language shows that there are those who, in obedience to Christ, are willing to forsake the fulfillment of the flesh in sex, intimacy in marriage, and the joy in having children. If they do this for Christ and for the service of the gospel, they should be honored for their sacrifice. Jesus does not hesitate to honor such people. Neither should we.

Question 22: If a transgender individual gets saved, should the church require them to undergo a restorative sex change operation so that they are anatomically their original gender?

Eventually, every church in the United States and Western Europe will face a question like this. The first thing we must remember is that the gospel is for everyone—regardless of gender identity. The gospel is for the transgender and the transsexual just as much as it is for the one who identifies with his birth gender.

The gospel promises wholeness in Christ and calls us to holiness. Thus, in response to the gospel, all true Christians seek to live in obedience to the God who created us male and female. Obedience to Christ means that we seek in every way to progressively move toward embracing our birth gender rather than lingering in rebellion or confusion.

This is not to suggest that the progress of sanctification is easy or instantaneous. As Eugene Peterson said, the Christian life is "a long obedience in the same direction."[4] In other words, obedience can be slow progress.

What if the individual had undergone medical procedures and sex change operations before coming to Christ? Would surgery now be pastorally required or advisable in order to obey Christ? This situation requires the loving council of a local church to help this particular Christian understand what "long obedience" in this circumstance would involve. Pastors and congregations should consider age, context, and even physical and physiological factors when determining a course of action. But even without surgery, Christians in this situation should publicly and privately identify themselves according to their birth gender. Surgery is a secondary question to be handled with pastoral wisdom and sound medical advice.

Question 23: What is the relationship between body and gender? Does anatomy determine gender?

Modern brain research suggests that the brains of men and women have some crucial differences. But the essential biological gender identity is established by physiological realities that are, in the vast majority of human beings, immediately identifiable upon birth. When a baby is born, physically identified, and declared to be a boy or a girl, this is an affirmation of God's lifelong purpose for that individual. The Bible tells us the body reveals identity to us in that respect and in others as well.

For a very small portion of people, only about one in every fifteen hundred births, the birth gender is indeterminate. These individuals are now most often medically referred to as *intersex*. This birth anomaly—which is identified by medical science as an anomaly—requires the parents first and the individual later to make some essential choices. These choices are matters not of obedience versus disobedience, but of wisdom and mercy. In such cases, we must always strive for the good of the individual. This issue is not the same as rejecting one's clear biological sex. These are different issues and call for a different pattern of response.[5]

Question 24: Aren't laws that give Christians the right to refuse goods and services to a same-sex couple for their wedding similar to Jim Crow laws?

Same-sex marriage proponents want us to believe that sexual orientation is morally equivalent to race. This is the logic they have been successful in advocating. They believe that discrimination on the basis of sexual orientation equates to discrimination on the basis of race or ethnicity. If this is right, then Christians must condemn refusing to provide flowers for a same-sex wedding as sin just as they would condemn refusing to provide flowers for an interracial wedding as sin.

But sexual orientation is not the same thing as race. The reality is that people in countless businesses are now being coerced into approving the moral status of same-sex relationships because they are being forced to participate. Most of these businesses would not discriminate against same-sex couples or individuals in general, but only when participation would require them to make a moral statement that violates their Christian commitments. Refusing to bake a cake with a message celebrating a same-sex marriage is simply not the same thing as refusing to seat a same-sex couple for dinner. One is an act of despicable discrimination. The other is an act consistent with religious conviction concerning the nature of marriage and sexual morality.

Question 25: Homosexuals testify that marriage makes them happier and does not hurt anyone, so how can this be wrong?

One of the most dangerous ideas about today's morality is the suggestion that we should limit human behavior only on the basis of identifiable harm. Reducing morality to the avoidance of harm is dangerous because it tends to reduce harm to that which is immediately identifiable in an individual's experience or in society at large.

Legalizing same-sex marriage does not mean the heterosexual couple next door will experience immediate harm. It does mean marriage as an institution is harmed, however, which weakens the social cohesiveness and health of the entire society. The problem with arguments concerning the morality of harm is that much of what causes the most devastating and lasting harm is not readily apparent. In many aspects, the law recognizes that reality by establishing patterns of right behavior. The violation of these patterns would cause no immediate harm to a specific individual, but the lack of them would weaken the entire society.

Question 26: Should the government legislate morality?

Every government legislates morality because every law has some identifiable moral purpose. Even administrative laws and traffic ordinances have a moral agenda to ensure public safety, promote order, and prevent accidents. Yet the most contentious and central issues of the law are so steeped in morality that it is foolish to suggest that the government should not legislate morality. Laws prohibiting theft, murder, assault, rape, and kidnapping make a strong moral judgment rooted in a clear moral consensus. These laws legislate morality.

When someone argues that the government should not legislate morality, the limiting of a specific personal behavior—especially sexual behavior—is almost always the issue. Yet the law will always legislate morality, even if it refuses to legislate on a specific issue. Removing legislation or declining legislation is always a political act with moral implications, just as refusing to vote in a democratic election is a political act with moral implications. When it comes to legislating morality—whether the issue is sex or some other lifestyle issue—every sane, stable, lasting society legislates vast areas of morality. Even when moral issues are not made matters of legislation, they remain a matter of cultural decision, social responsibility, and moral consequence.

Question 27: Should the government play any role in legislating marriage?

In some sense, this question seems to assume that churches have been in the marriage business all along and that the secular state is the latecomer. But human history and virtually every human society shows that civil marriage has always been an interest to all human governments. Furthermore, marriage is pre-political. The government recognizes marriage as the most basic molecular structure of society; thus, every government has historically privileged and protected marriage as the union of a man and a woman. In order to preserve society and its interests, governments must honor the marital covenant, promote procreation, and encourage parents in child rearing.

When the first colonies were established in America, marriage was considered a civil institution. Some Puritans did not even see marriage as the ceremonial responsibility of the church. It now appears inevitable that the faithful church will operate by a more restrictive definition of marriage than the larger culture will operate. Government, however, can never get out of the business of marriage or escape the responsibility of defining marriage, because government, by its very definition and nature, must determine who is accountable to whom, to whom children belong, who has the rights to make decisions on behalf of others, and what should be protected as the zone of intimate interest for the society itself.

Question 28: Should the church get out of the marriage business?

The church can certainly get out of the marriage business if the marriage business means the wedding business. The church can easily get out of the wedding business, but it cannot get out of responsibility for marriage. The church has a duty to uphold and honor marriage because Christ himself demonstrated the importance and centrality of marriage for human society. The New Testament reveals that the church must make decisions related to sexual morality, assign responsibility for the raising of children, outline distinctions within the household, and define the roles of a husband and wife. While these may not be interests of the state, they are inescapably interests of the church.

Question 29: If Christians press the state to recognize our view of marriage, aren't we forcing our religious commitments on society?

This would certainly be a legitimate argument if the Christian church independently came up with the definition of marriage as a heterosexual and monogamous covenant based on God's revelation in Scripture and then told secular society they had to agree with us. But that is both a legal and historical fiction. That conversation has never happened.

Secular society itself consistently defined marriage as the union of a man and a woman throughout millennia of human history. It often did so without any reference to Christianity, and, in most of the world, without any reference to the Bible. The notion of marriage as solely the union of a man and a woman is neither exclusively Christian nor exclusively biblical. Obedience to the Scripture means that believers cannot forfeit the definition of marriage found in Scripture, but civil societies around the world have not operated uniformly on the basis of Christian conviction. Nevertheless, they have—until recently—uniformly established marriage as the union of a man and a woman.

Question 30: Why should Christians care if same-sex couples marry? If they are unbelievers, why should Christians dictate their actions? Shouldn't we just worry about preaching the gospel?

This question is based upon the false premise that Scripture assigns the accountability to marriage to Christians alone rather than to society at large. Christian concern for marriage is deeply concerned with the moral risk taken by unbelievers when they marginalize, reject, subvert, or harm marriage in any way. Christians believe this risk threatens acting parties with eternal consequences.

Furthermore, it is quite selective and arbitrary to say that when it comes to same-sex marriage, Christians should not ask unbelievers to act like unbelievers. Why should that request be limited to same-sex marriage? Should it be applied to other aspects of the criminal code? Should Christians not expect non-Christians to live by the same civil laws they live by? Should Christians require non-Christians not to murder or steal? The law places demands on us on purpose. Laws exist because God gave the gift of law to human society for our protection and good, which are provided for both the believer and the unbeliever.

A WORD TO THE READER

As far as this Court is concerned, no one should be fooled; it
is just a matter of listening and waiting for the other shoe.
—Justice Antonin Scalia
Dissent to *Windsor* Decision,
June 26, 2013

Who do we think we are?
—Chief Justice John G. Roberts, Jr.
Dissent to *Obergefell* Decision
June 26, 2015

On June 26, 2015, the other shoe dropped. Two years to the day after
Justice Antonin Scalia warned that the legalization of same-sex marriage
would be inevitable, the Supreme Court did just as he predicted in its
decision in *Obergefell v. Hodges*. These pages are written in the immediate aftermath of that decision—a special addition to this book before
publication. We knew that the decision was coming, but it turned out to
be even more radical than we had feared.

Just weeks after the transgender revolution was announced on the
cover of *Vanity Fair* magazine, the Supreme Court of the United States
of America legally redefined marriage. Neither development came as a
surprise, but both are evidence of the tsunami-like moral revolution that
is reshaping our culture right before our eyes.

The majority's argument, expressed by Justice Kennedy, is that the right of same-sex couples to marry is based in individual autonomy as related to sexuality, in marriage as a fundamental right, in marriage as a privileged context for raising children, and in upholding marriage as central to civilization. But at every one of these points, the majority had to reinvent marriage in order to make its case. The court has not merely ordered that same-sex couples be allowed to marry—it has fundamentally redefined marriage itself.

The inventive legal argument set forth by the majority is clearly traceable in Justice Kennedy's previous decisions including *Lawrence* (2003) and *Windso*r (2013), and he cites his own decisions as legal precedent. As Chief Justice Roberts made clear, Justice Kennedy and his fellow justices in the majority wanted to legalize same-sex marriage and they invented a constitutional theory to achieve their purpose. It was indeed an act of will disguised as a legal judgment.

Justice Kennedy declared that "the right to marry is a fundamental right inherent in the liberty of the person, and under the Due Process and Equal Protection Clauses of the Fourteenth Amendment couples of the same-sex cannot be deprived of that right and that liberty." But marriage is nowhere to be found in the Constitution. As the Chief Justice asserted in his dissent, the majority opinion did not really make any serious constitutional argument at all. It was, as the Chief Justice insisted, an argument based in philosophy rather than in law.

The Supreme Court's overreach in this case is more astounding as the decision is reviewed in full, and as the dissenting justices voiced their own urgent concerns. The Chief Justice accused the majority of "judicial policymaking" that endangers our democratic form of government. "The Court today not only overlooks our country's entire history and tradition but actively repudiates it, preferring to live only in the heady days of the here and now," he asserted. Further: "Over and over, the majority exalts the role of the judiciary in delivering social change." Roberts went on to say, "The majority lays out a tantalizing vision for the future for Members of this Court. If an unvarying social institution enduring over all of recorded history cannot inhibit judicial policymaking, what can?" That is a haunting question. The Chief Justice's point is an urgent warning: if the Supreme Court will arrogate to itself the right to redefine marriage, there is no restraint on the judiciary whatsoever.

Justice Antonin Scalia offered a stinging rebuke to the majority. "This is a naked judicial claim to legislative—indeed super-legislative—power; a claim fundamentally at odds with our system of government," he stated. Justice Scalia then offered these stunning words of judgment: "A system of government that makes the people subordinate to a committee of nine unelected lawyers does not deserve to be called a democracy."

The Chief Justice also pointed to another very telling aspect of the majority opinion. The Kennedy opinion opens wide a door that basically invites looming demands for the legalization of polygamy and polyamory. As Chief Justice Roberts observed: "It is striking how much of the majority's reasoning would apply with equal force to the claim of a fundamental right to plural marriage." Striking, indeed. What is perhaps even more striking is that the majority did not even appear concerned about the extension of its logic to polygamy.

As the decision approached, those of us who have warned that the redefinition of marriage will not stop with same-sex unions were told that we were offering a fallacious slippery-slope argument. Now, the Chief Justice of the United States verifies that these concerns were fully valid. You can count on the fact that advocates for legalized polygamy found great encouragement in this decision.

The Supreme Court of the United States is the highest court in the land, and its decisions cannot be appealed to a higher court of law. But the Supreme Court, like every human institution and individual, will eventually face two higher courts. The first is the court of history, which will render a judgment that I believe will embarrass this court and reveal its dangerous trajectory. The precedents and arguments set forth in this decision cannot be limited to the right of same-sex couples to marry. If individual autonomy and equal protection mean that same-sex couples cannot be denied what is now defined as a fundamental right of marriage, then others will arrive to make the same argument. This court will find itself in a trap of its own making, and one that will bring great harm to this nation and its families. The second court we all must face is the court of divine judgment. For centuries, marriage ceremonies in the English-speaking world have included the admonition that what God has put together, no human being—or human court—should tear asunder. That is exactly what the Supreme Court of the United States has now done.

The threat to religious liberty represented by this decision is clear, present, and inevitable. Assurances to the contrary, the majority in this decision has placed every religious institution in legal jeopardy if that institution intends to uphold its theological convictions limiting marriage to the union of a man and a woman. This threat is extended to every religious citizen or congregation that would uphold the convictions held by believers for millennia. Justice Clarence Thomas warned in his dissent of "ruinous consequences for religious liberty."

One of the most dangerous dimensions of this decision is evident in what can only be described as the majority's vilification of those who hold to a traditional view of marriage as exclusively the union of a man and a woman. Justice Samuel Alito stated bluntly that the decision "will be used to vilify Americans who are unwilling to assent to the new orthodoxy." According to the argument offered by the majority, any opposition to same-sex marriage is rooted in moral animus against homosexuals. In offering this argument the majority slanders any defender of traditional marriage and openly rejects and vilifies those who, on the grounds of theological conviction, cannot affirm same-sex marriage.

In a very real sense, everything has now changed. The highest court of the land has redefined marriage. Those who cannot accept this re-definition of marriage as a matter of morality and ultimate truth, must acknowledge that the laws of this nation concerning marriage will indeed be defined against our will. We must acknowledge the authority of the Supreme Court in matters of law. Christians must be committed to be good citizens and good neighbors, even as we cannot accept this redefinition of marriage in our churches and in our lives.

We must contend for marriage as God's gift to humanity—a gift central and essential to human flourishing and a gift that is limited to the conjugal union of a man and a woman. We must contend for religious liberty for all, and focus our energies on protecting the rights of Christian citizens and Christian institutions to teach and operate on the basis of Christian conviction.

We cannot be silent, and we cannot join the moral revolution that stands in direct opposition to what we believe the Creator has designed, given, and intended for us. We cannot be silent, and we cannot fail to contend for marriage as the union of a man and a woman.

In one sense, everything has changed. And yet, nothing has changed. The cultural and legal landscape has changed, as we believe this will lead to very real harms to our neighbors. But our Christian responsibility has not changed. We are charged to uphold marriage as the union of a man and a woman and to speak the truth in love. We are also commanded to uphold the truth about marriage in our own lives, in our own marriages, in our own families, and in our own churches.

We are called to be the people of the truth, even when the truth is not popular and even when the truth is denied by the culture around us. Christians have found themselves in this position before, and we will again. God's truth has not changed. The holy Scriptures have not changed. The gospel of Jesus Christ has not changed. The church's mission has not changed. Jesus Christ is the same, yesterday, today, and forever.

ACKNOWLEDGMENTS

Writing is often a solitary act, but a book is never a purely individual accomplishment. I am acutely aware of that fact as I think of how many people have listened to me talk about these issues, how many books and writers have influenced my thinking, and how many kindnesses have been extended to me as this book was written.

I am deeply thankful to a crew of young seminary interns who work in my office and provide assistance in my research and writing. They also provide a constant stream of helpful conversation as we discuss everything from deep theological questions to the latest headlines. Each of them will make a mark in the world and faithfully serve the church: Duncan Collins, Jeremiah Greever, John Pendleton, Forrest Strickland, Andres Vera, and Chris Winegar.

Matt Tyler and Jon Swan worked to make sure I could find books in my own library (sometimes that is no small task). They love books, as do I, and they have helped to keep my library organized and happy.

Ryan Troglin, Jim Smith, and Jon Pentecost provided essential editing and Jon, who serves as producer of *The Briefing*, knew how to find any article I had cited on the program, even years after the fact.

My office would not have functioned without the excellent leadership of J. T. English and Tom Hellams, who both served as executive assistant to the president, among other duties, during the time the book was written. They both believed in the book, and it showed.

The book would not have been written on schedule and on point without the stellar assistance of Sam Emadi, director of theological research in my office. Working with Sam is a delight, and his commitment to scholarship was combined with his deep commitment to this project. He read my manuscripts before anyone else, and he has yet to make a suggestion that was not helpful.

I also appreciate Webster Younce, executive editor and associate publisher at Nelson Books—a publishing professional in every way—who also believed in this book and saw it through.

One of the greatest privileges of my life is to serve with the renowned faculty of the Southern Baptist Theological Seminary and Boyce College and to work with colleagues as committed and faithful as our executive cabinet. Dan Dumas and Randy Stinson, both senior vice presidents, are among those who have encouraged me at every point in the writing of this book. Faculty colleagues also encouraged me and, by their own faithfulness, make my role as president unspeakably fulfilling.

Finally, as at every point of my adult life, I thank the one person who has made the greatest contribution to everything I am and everything I do—Mary Mohler. She is not only my wife but my greatest encourager and constant friend. She put up with weeks of walking around a staircase stacked with books and articles, organized chapter by chapter. She endured months of writing and editing. I don't believe there is anything she would not do for me, and I constantly seem to test that theory. She is simply magnificent.

NOTES

Chapter 1: In the Wake of a Revolution

1. Flannery O'Connor, *The Habit of Being: The Letters of Flannery O'Connor,* ed. Sally Fitzgerald (New York: Farrar, Straus, Giroux, 1979), 229.

2. Theo Hobson, "A Pink Reformation," *The Guardian,* February 5, 2007, http://www.theguardian.com/commentisfree/2007/feb/05/apinkreformation/.

3. Ibid.

4. Ibid.

5. Carl F. H. Henry, *God, Revelation, and Authority,* vol. 6, *God Who Stands and Says, Part 2* (Wheaton: Crossway, 1999), 454.

6. Charles Taylor, *A Secular Age* (Cambridge: The Belknap Press of Harvard University Press, 2007).

7. Mary Eberstadt, *How the West Really Lost God: A New Theory of Secularization* (West Conshohocken, PA: Templeton Press, 2013), 38.

8. Claire Suddath with Duane Stanford, "Coke Confronts Its Big Fat Problem," *Bloomberg Buisnessweek,* July 31, 2014, http://www.bloomberg.com/bw/articles/2014-07-31/coca-cola-sales-decline-health-concerns-spur-relaunch/.

9. Pitirim Sorokin, *The American Sex Revolution* (Boston: Porter Sargent, 1956), 1.

10. The actual term "sexual revolution" can be traced to an Austrian writer, Wilhelm Reich, who was one of the intellectuals pushing this idea of a revolution in sexual morality. Wilhelm Reich, *The Sexual Revolution,* trans. Therese Pol (New York: Farrar, Straus & Giroux, 1974).

11. Lillian B. Rubin, *Erotic Wars: What Happened to the Sexual Revolution?* (New York: Farrar, Straus & Giroux, 1990), 9.

12. Alfred C. Kinsey, *Sexual Behavior in the Human Male* (New York: Ishi

Press, 2010); and *Sexual Behavior in the Human Female* (New York: Ishi Press, 2010). Also see the chapter concerning Kinsey in R. Albert Mohler Jr., *Desire and Deceit: The Real Cost of the New Sexual Tolerance* (Colorado Springs: Multnomah, 2008), 103–12.

13. Sue Ellin Browder, "Kinsey's Secret: The Phony Science of the Sexual Revolution." *Crisis Magazine*, May 28, 2012, http://www.crisismagazine.com /2012/kinseys-secret-the-phony-science-of-the-sexual-revolution/.

14. See the Pew Forum on Religion & Public Life, *"Nones" on the Rise: One-in-Five Adults Have No Religious Affiliation,"* (Washington, DC: Pew Research Center, October 9, 2012), http://www.pewforum.org/files/2012/10/Nones OnTheRise-full.pdf.

15. John Heidenry, *What Wild Ecstasy: The Rise and Fall of the Sexual Revolution* (New York: Simon & Schuster, 1997), 414.

Chapter 2: It Didn't Start with Same-Sex Marriage

1. Margaret Sanger, *The Pivot of Civilization* (New York: Brentano's, 1922; reprint ed., Teddington, Middlesex, UK: Echo Library, 2006).

2. Similarly, most evangelicals are today quite unaware of the fact that the Pill, though legal in the early 1960s, was generally only prescribed to married women in an effort to limit increased promiscuity. In terms of American history, most Americans would be surprised to know that the first president of the United States to speak positively of birth control was Lyndon Johnson in the mid-1960s.

3. *Griswold v. Connecticut*, 381 U.S. 479 (1965).

4. Pat Conroy, "Anatomy of a Divorce," *Atlanta*, November 1, 1978, http:// www.atlantamagazine.com/great-reads/anatomy-of-a-divorce/.

5. Jason DeParle and Sabrina Tavernise, "For Women Under 30, Most Births Occur Outside Marriage," *New York Times*, February 17, 2012, www.nytimes .com/2012/02/18/us/for-women-under-30-most-births-occur-outside-marriage .html. Just two days after the publication of that report, the same newspaper declared that "out-of-wedlock births are the new normal" for younger mothers. See KJ Dell'Antonia, "For Younger Mothers, Out-of-Wedlock Births Are the New Normal," *Motherlode* (blog), February 19, 2012, http:// parenting.blogs.nytimes.com/2012/02/19/for-younger-mothers-out-of -wedlock-births-are-the-new-normal/.

6. DeParle and Tavernise, "For Women Under 30."

7. Ibid. Interestingly, this article also tied this news to the larger context of the

sexual revolution. As the paper noted, "The forces rearranging the family are as diverse as globalization and the pill. Liberal analysts argue that shrinking paychecks have thinned the ranks of marriageable men." On the other hand, conservatives argue that "the sexual revolution reduced the incentive to wed and that safety net programs discourage marriage." Actually, faced with this evidence, both conservatives and liberals should agree with the truth of the other party's case. There are both economic and moral considerations in play here, but economics is never without connection to morality and morality is never without connection to cost.

8. Karen Benjamin Guzzo, "Trends in Cohabitation Outcomes: Compositional Changes and Engagement Among Never-Married Young Adults," *Journal of Marriage and Family* 76, no. 4 (August 2014): 827.

9. See also R. Albert Mohler, "Sin by Survey? Americans Say What They Think," AlbertMohler.com, March 20, 2008, http://www.albertmohler.com/2008/03/20/sin-by-survey-americans-say-what-they-think/.

10. Tom W. Smith in "Where Are We and How Did We Get Here?" in *Marriage—Just a Piece of Paper?*, ed. Katherine Anderson, Don Browning, and Brian Boyer (Grand Rapids: Eerdmans, 2002), 26.

Chapter 3: From Vice to Virtue: How Did the Homosexual Movement Happen?

1. Kevin Phillips, *American Theocracy: The Peril and Politics of Radical Religion, Oil, and Borrowed Money in the 21st Century* (New York: Penguin, 2006), 241.

2. See Gallup, "Gay and Lesbian Rights," Gallup.com, http://www.gallup.com/poll/1651/gay-lesbian-rights.aspx; Lydia Saad, "Americans Evenly Divided on Morality of Homosexuality," Gallup.com, June 18, 2008, http://www.gallup.com/poll/108115/americans-evenly-divided-morality-homosexuality.aspx; the Pew Research Center for the People & the Press and Pew Forum on Religion & Public Life, "Majority Continues to Support Civil Unions," Pew Research Center, October 9, 2009, http://www.pewforum.org/2009/10/09/majority-continues-to-support-civil-unions/.

3. See Robert P. Jones, et. al., "What Americans Want from Immigration Reform in 2014," Public Religion Research Institute, June 10, 2014; the Pew Forum on Religion & Public Life, "Section 3: Social and Political Issues," Pew Research Center, September 22, 2014, http://www.pewforum.org/2014/09/22/section-3-social-political-issues/; Justin McCarthy, "Same-Sex

Marriage Support Reaches New High at 55%," Gallup.com, May 21, 2014, http://www.gallup.com/poll/169640/sex-marriage-support-reaches-new -high.aspx.

4. It must be understood that pollsters and marketers are very aware of the fact that people responding to this kind of poll or survey often respond in a way that they believe the person asking the question would expect them or want them to respond. This kind of structural bias in polling suggests that even if a majority of Americans do not actually yet affirm the legalization of same-sex marriage, a majority now demonstrate that they believe they *should* be counted among those on the right side of the current cultural judgment.

5. Marshall Kirk and Hunter Madsen, *After the Ball: How America Will Conquer Its Fear & Hatred of Gays in the 90's* (New York: Doubleday, 1989), xxvii.

6. Ibid., 178.

7. Ibid., 179.

8. Ibid., 183.

9. Ibid., 184.

10. Ibid.

11. Ibid.

12. Ibid., 189–90.

13. Linda Hirshman, *Victory: The Triumphant Gay Revolution* (New York: Harper Perennial, 2013), 129.

14. David Eisenbach, *Gay Power: An American Revolution* (New York: Carroll & Graf, 2006), 231.

15. Ibid., 251.

16. At this point we must also note that the mainline Protestant denominations are disproportionately concentrated among the intellectual elites within American society. This is important since the precipitous decline in the membership and attendance in mainline Protestant churches is at least partially traced to the fact that the intellectual elites have become so secularized that they no longer feel any need to attend church—even a liberal church.

17. Brian D. McLaren, *A New Kind of Christianity: Ten Questions That Are Transforming the Faith* (New York: HarperCollins, 2010), 11.

18. Ibid., 180.

19. See "Brian McLaren on the Homosexual Question: Finding a Pastoral Response," PARSE, *Leadership Journal*, January 23, 2006, www.christianitytoday.com/parse /2006/january/brian-mclaren-on-homosexual-question-finding-pastoral.html/.

20. Ibid.

21. "Trevor McLaren and Owen Ryan," *New York Times*, September 23, 2012, http://www.nytimes.com/2012/09/23/fashion/weddings/trevor-mclaren-owen-ryan-weddings.html/.

22. Hirshman, *Victory*, 145.

23. Walter Frank, *Law and the Gay Rights Story: The Long Search for Equal Justice in a Divided Democracy* (New Brunswick, NJ: Rutgers University Press, 2014), 85.

24. Jo Becker, *Forcing the Spring: Inside the Fight for Marriage Equality* (New York: Penguin, 2014), 35.

25. The legal revolution that helped to drive the effort to normalize homosexuality is also traced very well by Leigh Ann Wheeler, *How Sex Became a Civil Liberty* (New York: Oxford University Press, 2013). But, as Wheeler tells the story, this did not begin with the effort to normalize homosexuality, but with the effort, undertaken by homosexuals, to push back on the traditional morality related to matters ranging from premarital sex and adultery to polyamory. In her convincing analysis, sex became a civil liberty because of the determined effort by sexual revolutionaries to use legal arguments to further their agenda. And, as she also documents with honesty, many of those activists were motivated by the effort to legalize, if not to normalize their own sexual practices.

26. Marco della Cava, "Hollywood: the best man of gay marriage," *USA Today*, June 26, 2013, http://usatoday30.usatoday.com/LIFE/usaedition/2013-06-27-Hollywood-eased-cultural-acceptance-of-marriage-ruling_ST_U.htm.

27. Ibid.

28. Ibid.

29. Ibid.

30. Quoted in Michael Medved, "Homosexuality and the Entertainment Media," *New Oxford Review* 68, no. 6 (June 2001): 37.

31. Ibid.

Chapter 4: The Impossible Possibility of Same-Sex Marriage

1. Interestingly, the call for the legalization of same-sex marriage largely came from figures that identified, in some way, with the cultural right in the United States and Great Britain. As members of the cultural right, these "gay conservatives" understood the utility and centrality of marriage to society and recognized the value of marriage as the primary context for human flourishing. Furthermore, they highly valued the social capital granted to married couples by the larger society—capital that includes a host of privileged recognitions and rights. While not all "gay conservatives" identify

with the assimilationist movement, their moral and political agenda is clearly to assimilate with the larger society by means of the institution of marriage.

2. William Eskridge, *The Case for Same-Sex Marriage: From Sexual Liberty to Civilized Commitment* (New York: Free Press, 1996).

3. Andrew Sullivan, *Virtually Normal: An Argument About Homosexuality* (New York: Alfred A. Knopf, 1995), 185.

4. Michelangelo Signorile, "I Do, I Do, I Do, I Do, I Do," *Out Magazine* (May 1996), 30.

5. Ibid., 32.

6. Ibid., 113.

7. See the Pew Forum on Religion & Public Life, *"Nones" on the Rise: One-in-Five Adults Have No Religious Affiliation,"* (Washington, DC: Pew Research Center, October 9, 2012), http://www.pewforum.org/files/2012/10/Nones OnTheRise-full.pdf.

8. James Davison Hunter, *To Change the World: The Irony, Tragedy, & Possibility of Christianity in the Late Modern World* (Oxford: Oxford University Press, 2010), 41.

9. Sherif Girgis, Ryan T. Anderson, and Robert P. George, *What Is Marriage? Man and Woman: A Defense* (New York: Encounter Books, 2011).

10. Ibid., 1.

11. Ibid., 69.

Chapter 5: The Transgender Revolution

1. Jennifer Finney Boylan, "I Had a Boyhood, Once," *New York Times*, July 20, 2014, http://www.nytimes.com/2014/07/21/opinion/boylan-boyhood-the -better-angels.html. Boylan, a professor of English at Barnard College, also documents her transgendered experience in her book *Stuck in the Middle with You: Parenthood in Three Genders* (New York: Crown, 2013).

2. Katy Steinmetz, "The Transgender Tipping Point," *Time*, May 29, 2014, http://time.com/135480/transgender-tipping-point/.

3. Ibid.

4. See, for example, Joanne Meyerowitz, *How Sex Changed: A History of Transsexuality in the United States* (Cambridge, MA: Harvard University Press, 2004), 285. "The rise of the transgender movement capped the century in which sex change first became a medical specialty and transsexuals first emerged as a visible social group. From the early twentieth-century experiments on changing the sex of animals to the liberationist

movement of the 1990s, the topic of sex change had served as a key site for the definition and redefinition of sex in popular culture, science, medicine, law, and daily life. In a century when others had challenged the social categories and hierarchies of class, race, and gender, the people who hoped to change their sex had brought into question another fundamental category—biological sex itself—commonly understood as obvious and unchangeable."

5. Human Rights Campaign Foundation, "A Few Definitions for Educators and Parents/Guardians," Welcoming Schools website, accessed April 28, 2015, http://www.welcomingschools.org/pages/a-few-definitions-for-educators -and-parents-guardians.

6. Ibid.

7. See, for example, the comments by Lori B. Gershick, *Transgender Voices: Beyond Women and Men* (Lebanon, NH: University Press of New England, 2008), 5. "I believe in the social construction of reality. What we believe—how we think about ourselves, our relationships, our social world—has less to do with scientific or biological 'facts' and more to do with profound familial, cultural, and social training that reinforces what is considered 'normal.' Whether or not 'normal' defines real experience for a few, many, or anyone doesn't much matter. What does matter is that 'normal' maintains a set of hierarchical political structures, economic systems, and social conventions that benefit those at the top of the pyramid."

8. The Evangelical Women's Caucus was established to advocate feminist concerns within the evangelical movement. It divided after years of acrimony over the question of lesbianism. See S. Sue Horner, "Trying to Be God in the World: The Story of the Evangelical Women's Caucus and the Crisis over Homosexuality," in *Gender, Ethnicity, and Religion: Views from the Other Side*, ed. Rosemary Radford Ruether (Minneapolis: Fortress Press, 2002), 99–124.

9. Virginia Ramey Mollenkott, *Omnigender: A Trans-Religious Approach* (Cleveland: Pilgrim Press, 2007), 8. "People who dislike my proposal of an omnigender social construct will no doubt do so out of loyalty to the idea that there really is an essential feminine and masculine binary that is either God's will or nature's perpetual norm or both. Ironically, they will cling to this essentialist gender construct by denying that gender *is* socially constructed in any way."

10. Ibid., 166.

11. Ibid., 167.

12. Ibid., 168.

13. Ibid.
14. Ibid., 169.
15. Ibid.
16. The text of this e-mail can be found at: http://thefederalist.com/wp-content
    /uploads/2014/08/JanneyEmail.pdf. This link is provided by Mary Hasson
    in "Back to School: When Mr. Reuter Becomes 'Ms. Reuter,'" *The Federalist*,
    August 5, 2014, http://thefederalist.com/2014/08/05/back-to-school-when-mr
    -reuter-becomes-ms-reuter/.
17. Human Rights Campaign Foundation, "A Few Definitions for Educators
    and Parents/Guardians."
18. Hasson, "Back to School: When Mr. Reuter Becomes 'Ms. Reuter.'" The
    transgender revolution is also trying to push the relevant age for first dealing
    with the gender question all the way back to birth. A rather stunning article
    by Christin Scarlett Milloy argues that the infliction of biological sex upon an
    infant is a form of cruelty. In her words: "With infant gender assignment, at
    a single moment your baby's life is instantly and brutally reduced from such
    infinite potentials down to one concrete set of expectations and stereotypes,
    and any behavioral deviation from that will be severely punished—both
    intentionally through bigotry, and unintentionally through ignorance. That
    doctor (and the power structure behind him) plays a pivotal role in imposing
    those limits on helpless infants, without their consent, and without your
    informed consent as a parent. This issue deserves serious consideration by
    every parent, because no matter what gender identity your child ultimately
    adopts, infant gender assignment has effects that will last throughout their
    whole life." See Christin Scarlett Milloy, "Don't Let the Doctor Do This to
    Your Newborn," *Outward* (blog), June 26, 2014, http://www.slate.com/blogs
    /outward/2014/06/26/infant_gender_assignment_unnecessary_and_potentially
    _harmful.html.
19. Steinmetz, "The Transgender Tipping Point."
20. Michael Kiefer, "Arizona Appeals Court: 'Pregnant Man' can get a divorce,"
    Arizona Republic, August 14, 2014, http://www.azcentral.com/story/news
    /local/arizona/2014/08/13/arizona-appeals-court-pregnant-man-can-get
    -divorce/14026193/.
21. Sarah Pulliam Bailey, "H. Adam Ackley, Transgender Theology Professor,
    Asked to Leave California's Azusa Pacific University," *Huffington Post*,
    September, 23, 2013, http://www.huffingtonpost.com/2013/09/23/transgender
    -professor-azusa-pacific-_n_3977109.html.

22. Lila Shapiro, "Domaine Javier, Transgender Student, Sues University That Expelled Her For 'Fraud,'" *Huffington Post*, February 27, 2013, http://www .huffingtonpost.com/2013/02/27/domaine-javier-lawsuit_n_2775756.html.

23. Allan Metcalf, "LGBTQQ2IA," *Lingua Franca* (a blog of the *Chronicle of Higher Education*), August 19, 2014, http://chronicle.com/blogs/linguafranca/2014/08 /19/lgbtqq2ia/.

24. Ibid.

25. Ibid.

26. Ibid.

27. Allan Metcalf, "What's Your PGP?," *Lingua Franca* (a blog of the *Chronicle of Higher Education*), September 2, 2014, http://chronicle.com/blogs/ linguafranca/2014/09/02/whats-your-pgp/.

28. Gay Straight Alliance for Safe Schools, "What the heck is a 'PGP'?" http:// www.gsafewi.org/wp-content/uploads/What-the-heck-is-a-PGP1.pdf.

29. "Faculty guide to working with Transgender & Gender Non-Conforming students in the classroom," Central Connecticut State University LGBT Center, accessed April 1, 2015, http://web.ccsu.edu/lgbtcenter/facGuides.asp; "Name, Pronoun, & Gender Marker Changes," University of Colorado at Boulder GLBTQ Resource Center, accessed April 1, 2015, http://www .colorado.edu/glbtqrc/name-pronoun-gender-marker-changes.

30. Denny Burk, *What Is the Meaning of Sex?* (Wheaton, IL: Crossway, 2013), 160.

31. McHugh's final analysis is even more straightforward and important. He argued that changing sex is ultimately "impossible." "People who undergo sex-reassignment surgery do not change from men to women, or vice versa. Rather, they become feminized men or masculinized women. Claiming that this is a civil-rights matter and encouraging surgical intervention is in reality to collaborate with and promote a mental disorder." Paul McHugh, "Transgender Surgery Isn't the Solution," *Wall Street Journal*, June 12, 2014.

Chapter 6: The End of Marriage

1. Renee Ellis and Rose M. Kreider, *Number, Timing, and Duration of Marriages and Divorces: 2009*, United States Census Bureau, May 2011, http://www.census.gov/prod/2011pubs/p70–125.pdf.; Dan Hurley, "Divorce Rate: It's Not as High as You Think," *New York Times,* April 19, 2005, http://www.nytimes.com/2005/04/19 /health/19divo.html?_r=0.; D'Vera Cohn, "At Long Last, Divorce," Pew Research Center, June 4, 2010, http:// www.pewresearch.org/2010/06/04/at-long-last-divorce/.

2. Brigitte Berger and Peter Berger, *The War Over the Family: Capturing the Middle Ground* (New York: Anchor Press/Doubleday, 1983), 4.

3. Christopher Lasch, *Haven in a Heartless World: The Family Besieged* (New York: Basic Books, 1977).

4. Donald S. Browning, *Marriage and Modernization: How Globalization Threatens Marriage and What to Do About It* (Grand Rapids: Eerdmans, 2003), 18.

5. Mark Regnerus, "How Different Are Adult Children of Parents Who Have Same-Sex Relationships? Findings from the New Family Structures Study," *Social Science Research* 41 (2012): 752–70.

6. "Beyond Same-Sex Marriage: A New Strategic Vision for All Our Families and Relationships," Beyond Marriage, last modified July 26, 2006, http://beyondmarriage.org/full_statement.html.

7. Ibid.

8. Judith Stacey, *Unhitched: Love, Marriage, and Family Values from West Hollywood to Western China* (New York: NYU Press, 2012), 151.

Chapter 7: What Does the Bible Really Have to Say About Sex?

1. Carl F. H. Henry, *God, Revelation, and Authority, Vol. 3: The God Who Speaks and Shows* (Wheaton: Crossway, 1999), 405.

2. The "theology of the body" was courageously advocated by Pope John Paul II, who frankly and compassionately defended both marriage and the sanctity of life.

3. Those who are born intersex or identified as hermaphroditic are obviously human beings made in the image of God, along with every other member of the human family. We must also assert that in the rare cases in which a child is born with indefinite gender, it should be left to parents and medical practitioners to suggest the means whereby that child can be assisted toward the greatest happiness and flourishing. At the same time, reference to intersex individuals or those of indeterminate sex by those pushing for the transgender revolution is a fallacious argument. Christians should understand that, even as every one of us is born broken, that brokenness is evidenced in every human being in different ways. For those born with indeterminate gender, that very fact is evidence, not of their own unique brokenness, but of the brokenness of the cosmos. These difficult issues point to our only hope of ultimate wholeness and restoration through the atonement of the Lord Jesus Christ.

4. J. Gresham Machen, "The Separateness of the Church," in *God Transcendent*, by Ned Bernard Stonehouse (Edinburgh: Banner of Truth Trust, 1982), 113.

5. Dan O. Via and Robert A. J. Gagnon, *Homosexuality and the Bible: Two Views* (Minneapolis: Fortress Press, 2003), 94.

6. From the statement by William M. Kent published in *Report of the Committee to Study Homosexuality to the General Council on Ministries of the United Methodist Church*, August 24, 1991.

7. Matthew Vines, *God and the Gay Christian: The Biblical Case in Support of Same-Sex Relationships* (Colorado Springs: Convergent Books, 2014). My colleagues and I responded to Vines's book in *God and the Gay Christian: A Response to Matthew Vines*, ed. R. Albert Mohler Jr. (Louisville: SBTS Press, 2014), http://126df895942e26f6b8a0-6b5d65e17b10129dda21364daca4 e1f0.r8.cf1.rackcdn.com/GGC-Book.pdf.

8. Vines, *God and the Gay Christian*, 130. Emphasis in original.

9. Ibid., 102.

10. Ibid., 130.

11. Ibid., 2.

12. See E. Michael Jones, *Degenerate Moderns: Modernity as Rationalized Sexual Misbehavior* (San Francisco: Ignatius Press, 1993).

Chapter 8: Religious Liberty and the Right to Be Christian

1. See "No Right to Refuse Gay Couple's Wedding Cake," *Denver Post*, December 9, 2013, http://www.denverpost.com/editorials/ci_24687970/no-right-refuse -gay-couples-wedding-cake/. Mollie Ziegler Hemingway, "Gay Marriage Collides with Religious Liberty," *Wall Street Journal*, September 19, 2013, http://online.wsj.com/news/articles/SB1000142412788732466560457908171 42146908298/.

2. The Supreme Court of the State of New Mexico, *Elane Photography, LLC v. Vanessa Willock,* August 22, 2013, Docket No. 33, 687, http://online.wsj .com/public/resources/documents/Photogopinion.pdf.

3. Marc D. Stern, "Same-Sex Marriage and the Churches," in *Same-Sex Marriage and Religious Liberty: Emerging Conflicts*, eds. Douglas Laycock, Anthony R. Picarello Jr., and Robin Fretwell Wilson (Lanham, MD: Rowman & Littlefield, 2008), 1.

4. Ibid., 57.

5. Chai R. Feldblum, "Moral Conflict and Conflicting Liberties," in Douglas Laycock, Anthony R. Picarello, and Robin Fretwell Wilson, *Same-Sex Marriage and Religious Liberty: Emerging Conflicts*, 124–125.

6. Ibid., 125.

7. *Planned Parenthood of Southeastern Pennsylvania v. Casey*, 505 U.S. 833 (1992).

8. See, for example, Frank Bruni's article where he says, "I support the right of people to believe what they do and say what they wish—in their pews, homes and hearts" (Frank Bruni, "Your God and My Dignity: Religious Liberty, Bigotry and Gays," *New York Times*, January 10, 2015, http://mobile.nytimes .com/2015/01/11/opinion/sunday/frank-bruni-religious-liberty-bigotry-and -gays.html?smprod=nytcore-iphone&smid=nytcore-iphone-share&_r=4 &referrer=.

9. Subpoena available at http://www.adfmedia.org/files/WoodfillSubpoena Request.pdf.

10. Katie Leslie, "Atlanta Fire Chief Suspended Over Book Controversy," *Atlanta Journal-Constitution*, Monday, November 24, 2014.

11. *United States v. Windsor*, 570 U.S. ___ (2013).

12. Jonathan Rauch, *Kindly Inquisitors: The New Attacks on Free Thought* (Chicago: University of Chicago Press, 2013), 179.

13. Ibid., 181.

Chapter 9: The Compassion of Truth: The Church and the Challenge of the Sexual Revolution

1. See R. Albert Mohler Jr., "The Giglio Imbroglio—The Public Inauguration of a New Moral McCarthyism," AlbertMohler.com, January 10, 2013, hhttp://www .albertmohler.com/2013/01/10/the-giglio-imbroglio-the-public-inauguration -of-a-new-moral-mccarthyism/

2. Lord Alfred Douglas, "Two Loves," Poets.org, accessed May 28, 2015, http://www.poets.org/poetsorg/poem/two-loves.

3. Christian Smith, *Soul Searching: The Religious and Spiritual Lives of American Teenagers* (Oxford: Oxford University Press, 2005), 162.

4. Ibid., 162–63.

5. Christian Smith, *Souls in Transition: The Religious & Spiritual Lives of Emerging Adults* (Oxford: Oxford University Press, 2009), 81.

6. David Kinnaman and Gabe Lyons, *Unchristian: What a New Generation Really Thinks about Christianity . . . and Why It Matters* (Grand Rapids: Baker, 2007), 92.

7. David Kinnaman, *You Lost Me: Why Young Christians Are Leaving Church . . . and Rethinking Faith* (Grand Rapids: Baker, 2011), 22.

8. Carl Trueman, professor of theology and church history at Westminster Theological Seminary in Philadelphia, recently declared: "We live in a time of exile. At least those of us do who hold to traditional Christian beliefs.

The strident rhetoric of scientism has made belief in the supernatural look ridiculous. The Pill, no-fault divorce, and now gay marriage have made traditional sexual ethics look outmoded at best and hateful at worst. The Western public square is no longer a place where Christians feel they belong with any degree of comfort." His words are profoundly true. Carl Trueman, "A Church for Exiles," *First Things*, http://www.firstthings.com/article/2014 /08/a-church-for-exiles.

9. Carl F. H. Henry, *Evangelicals in Search of Identity* (Waco, TX: Word, 1976), 16.

Chapter 10: The Hard Questions

1. See Robert A. J. Gagnon, *The Bible and Homosexual Practice: Texts and Hermeneutics* (Nashville: Abingdon Press, 2002).

2. See the discussion of this issue in chapter 7 of this book.

3. Historically, the argument for this notion in the public square can be traced back to Simon LeVay and others who claimed to discover a gay gene, but other scientists have not confirmed LeVay's research.

4. Eugene Peterson, *A Long Obedience in the Same Direction: Discipleship in an Instant Society* (Wheaton, IL: InterVarsity Press, 2000).

5. See the discussion of the same issue in chapter 5 of this book.

INDEX

ABOUT THE AUTHOR

R. Albert Mohler, Jr., is president of the Southern Baptist Theological Seminary and the Joseph Emerson Brown Professor of Christian Theology. Considered a leader among American evangelicals by *Time* and *Christianity Today* magazines, Dr. Mohler can be heard on *The Briefing*, a daily podcast that analyzes news and events from a Christian worldview. He also writes a popular commentary on moral, cultural, and theological issues at albertmohler.com. He and his family live in Louisville, Kentucky.